one
Changing the World from the Inside Out

Noj Hinkins

Editor and co-creator
Liz Blossom

Iceberg Coaching

First published in the United Kingdom in 2010 by Iceberg Coaching

ISBN 978-0-9564291-0-0

This book has been printed on paper that is sourced
and harvested from sustainable forests.

Contents

Preface

Has this book unexpectedly come into your life?

Do the circumstances surrounding the fact that you are looking at this page seem random?

They are not.

This is no coincidence.

The reason that you are reading these exact words at this exact moment in time involves the evolution of both the human race at large and you as an individual. Whether you know it or not, the choices you have made and the things you have said and done have led to this being the perfect moment for you to read these words. You have created this moment, this opportunity. It is now up to you what you do with it.

A fundamental change in the way people see the world is occurring and it will enable people to achieve more than they ever dreamed possible. This is your invitation to gain awareness of that shift in consciousness. Once you have gained awareness of the One perspective, you will be set up to unleash the power of your true potential on the world. But be warned; it is not an easy journey.

You now have a choice.

You can take on the last great adventure of mankind – the ultimate voyage of self-discovery – and begin the journey towards realising your highest potential. There are no guarantees and it may be a rocky road on the way to rejoicing in the highs. You may end up leading an incredibly fulfilling life, every day. You will not only discover the meaning of life, but also your integral part in the next evolutionary step for mankind.

Or you can choose to close the book. The time may not be right for you now and that's fine ... really it is.

Whatever you choose, I believe it will be the right decision for you.

Welcome to One.

Introduction

The Unique Opportunity of our Time

We are at a unique point in history. In the West two generations have lived in peace for the first time ever. Unprecedented advances in technology have occurred. The demands on people who want to be successful are dramatically different now compared to any other stage in the evolution of our species. This brave new world comes with incredible possibility and potential, the likes of which we have never seen before.

It also comes with significant dangers. The evolution of our behaviour is lagging behind the evolution of the modern world with its emphasis on speed, technology and appearances. That is creating stress. If you put a frog in a pot of boiling water, it will leap out. But if you put it in a pan of cold water and slowly heat it, the frog will stay put even when the water reaches boiling point. It is the same with us. Each imperceptible change that occurs does not seem too different from the last, but the heat is rising. We are in danger of being boiled alive unless we adapt and change too. The problem is that we look around us at all the other 'frogs' and think to ourselves, 'It feels a bit hot, but they are still sitting in here, so it must be OK.'

But things are now getting out of control. 'Modern life' has been out of balance for too long and things are getting worse as the heat rises. The World Health Organization (WHO) has recently predicted that the second highest contributor to disease burden in 2020 will be depression.[1] Depression and its related cousin stress are our modern world's boiling water and they are spreading like wildfire. If we can adapt and change our behaviour, we can leap out of the water before it boils and unleash the power of our true potential on the world. The prospective rewards for you are incredible.

The stakes are high. Front page headlines tell us that over a million children in the UK (that's 1 in 10 between the ages of five and sixteen) have mental health problems such as depression, anxiety, anorexia and violent delinquency.[2] We are also sitting in the midst of one of the earth's great mass extinctions and global warming is not just a future theory, but a here and now reality. By 2020, the world's population will have tripled in only one generation. This coincides with the WHO prediction of a huge increase in rates of depression.

We are poised at a high-risk decision point. This book is about awareness of the choices that now face us. In line with the advances in technology, some incredible discoveries are taking place, the potential implications of which are staggering. For the first time in human history the latest scientific understanding and ancient spiritual beliefs are beginning to collide. As a result we are approaching an important moment that will define a generation. As I write this, awareness of what is happening is limited, but the time has come for a landslide change in our perception of how the world operates.

This book comes in two parts. The first part explains the three cornerstones of this alternative perspective on the world along with examples and exercises to bring it to life. Developing awareness of this perspective gives a new context to our behaviour. Adopting this new paradigm is mankind's next challenging step in the evolution of its species. The second part takes that perspective and makes it personal to you. It acts as a guide to unleashing the power of your true potential. Taking on this journey is the next challenging step in the personal evolution of your self. These two parallel journeys of self and society are inextricably linked. We are all in it together.

The main purpose of this book is to spread awareness. I am writing this book to be read by you – an adult whom I believe to be creative, resourceful and whole. I hold you and your points of view in high regard. You may agree or disagree with what is written here and that is fine. I just think you should be aware of what is happening so that you can make conscious decisions about how you want to live your life in this brave new world. This book is nothing without you. You will decide what you do with it and its message. You will determine what happens next.

Simplicity

I am not a great scholar and this book is designed to be readable rather than academic – rather like a chat we would have as friends. To that end this book will strive to adhere to the principle of simplicity. This book is intended to be a simple introduction to the new paradigm that anyone can understand. The main aim of this book is to spread awareness of what is happening for the good of individuals such as you, me and the rest of society.

I have had extensive experience working with people and organisations around the world. I have also backpacked around its edges. Along the way I have gathered a wealth of knowledge and experiences from every corner of the globe. From the frozen wastes of Antarctica to the oldest rainforest in the world; from indigenous tribes to multinational corporations; from ancient wisdom to cutting-edge physics. This book will show you how they all interlink and it will share some of the world's profound and inescapable truths.

There is too much in the world today that is great in theory, but of little use when it comes to real life. I believe that you want practical experiences to back up the theories. As a result, I promise that everything in this book is either a widely accepted fact or something I have witnessed in real life. I don't have time for ideas that sound good, but don't deliver the goods in the real world and I'm sure you are the same.

This book challenges many beliefs that are currently held about the way the world works and reveals why so many people are dissatisfied with the world at present. It also offers simple, pragmatic solutions that can enable you to unleash the power of your true potential. You may dramatically increase your personal happiness in the process of reading this book.

This book may well make you feel uncomfortable along the way. If it does, that is good – just be curious about why. Trying out new things is often accompanied by feelings of discomfort, but this discomfort inevitably leads to the greatest enlightenments. There will be many other people going through a similar journey. As you progress on this journey, you will start to meet them.

I am a coach and part of my role is to hold a mirror up to my clients in order to create self-awareness. I believe that with awareness comes 90% of the solution. Awareness is the platform for change. I intend this book to be a mirror for you so that you can become more aware of the way you operate and interact in the world. You may not like some of what you see. You may find that you are doing some things unconsciously because your parents did, your friends do or the people around you seem to demand it. Awareness of this will enable you to make some conscious choices about your future rather than living your life on 'default' settings.

To enable you to witness the reality of the book's central themes, a series of questions and challenges are posed throughout. I invite you to take some time out from reading this book periodically to observe the world through the One perspective and experience the reality for yourself. It helps to write down your findings in a notebook as there is something about writing things down that is invaluable. It makes your thoughts become real in the world and allows you to look back with clarity when the pressures of life and the mists of time have obscured the truth of the moment.

You may start your notebook with capturing, on a scale of 1–10, how committed you are to trying something new. Be honest. A low score will indicate that this book is likely to be an interesting read at most. An authentic high score indicates that you may just change your life during the course of reading this book.

It's all down to you.

You decide what happens next.

Part 1
The 'One' Perspective

Wake Up and Smell the New Coffee

What's a paradigm shift?

This book outlines a significant paradigm shift in the way we look at the world. A 'paradigm' is a generally held belief. A paradigm is backed up by so much evidence that it seems to everyone to be true ... well almost everyone. If people believe differently, if they can investigate it and prove a different way, then a paradigm shift occurs in them as they drop the old beliefs and adopt the new ones. If they can communicate this message effectively to the masses and if the masses on balance agree, then a significant paradigm shift occurs on a large scale.

A good example of a paradigm shift would be the change of view from the world being flat to it being round. A few hundred years ago many people thought that the world was flat. Gradually more and more scientific evidence came to light that caused a paradigm shift to the one we hold today – that the world is in fact round. Can you imagine what people must have thought back then as the idea that the world could be round started to emerge?

'The world is round? That's ridiculous!'
'How on earth would I be able to stand up on it if it was?'
'If the world was round, I would drop a ball and it would roll down the curve, but look – it doesn't happen.'
'Look outside! We can all see that the world is flat! Look at it!'
'It's not even worth spending my time trying to understand their preposterous theories.'

Even when people had sailed round the world, proving that it was round, when they returned there were many who would say:

'They are lying.'
'They mean well, they think that's what they have done, but they are deluded.'
'I won't believe it until I see it for myself ... but you won't catch me sailing off the horizon.'
'No one round here believes them, so why should I be any different?'
'What if they are wrong? Think what would happen! Better to play safe and stick with what you know.'

But of course now we know better ... although having said that, personally proving to an individual beyond a shadow of a doubt that the world is round is in fact very difficult. You would have to walk, sail or fly in a straight line, watching the compass all the time to be sure, but even then you would have to trust the compass. You could fly into space and look back down to earth, but even then you would have to trust that you were not part of an elaborate hoax.

To adopt a new paradigm there has to be an element of trust combined with enough evidence for you to see that there is something in it. Assuming that the One paradigm is justified, as you adopt it, just as much evidence will appear to prove your new beliefs as did to disprove it when you held the old paradigm. That is how it will be with this book. All I ask for is a little trust and that you give it a go. Most people have no idea of the amount of latent potential within them. I would love you to be able to unleash the power of your true potential on the world.

The suggestion of a new paradigm by its very nature seems absurd and ridiculous. If it didn't, everyone would have already adopted it. Today many individuals, from pioneers in scientific discovery to spiritual leaders, have already made a significant shift in the way they view the world. They already have enough personal and scientific evidence to adopt this mindset and are starting to reap the rewards of being leaders of the new paradigm as we speak. This book will show you the door through which they have passed and through which you may choose to pass if you want to join them.

This new paradigm shift is unlike any that has taken place in the history of mankind. Although over the centuries many people have witnessed the power of One, the technology and understanding was not available to fully explain it. As a result, the rights to it have often been claimed exclusively and people have been turned against one another in its name. There has never been a cohesive approach to bind its power so that humanity can pull in the same direction.

'One' combines centuries-old wisdom and contemporary discoveries in a way that enables people to see the truth behind human history. Once this next paradigm shift occurs, there will be no going back. The implications are enormous.

Before we get into the meat of exploring the One paradigm, let's begin by considering the kind of changes that will occur as awareness and adoption of the new paradigm increases.

The 'One World'

On a macro level, the big events that will be taking place will be positive breakthroughs. There will be significant leaps in the ability of individuals to understand each other. Focus will shift away from the past and towards the great possibility of the present moment resulting in peace where there were once never-ending cycles of war and bloodshed. Virtuous cycles will bind individuals from different backgrounds tightly together as they create trust, learn from each other and work together to maintain a new peaceful order that individuals are committed to maintaining.

Everything will be sustainable in the world. The environment will be safe in human hands with stable biodiversity throughout the world, populations of endangered species recovering and protected rainforests harvested for their medicinal products by locals. World trade will have evolved and stabilised to include fair trade for all and environmental degradation as well as poverty will be things of the past.

Without poverty and with a new breed of leaders, all nations will have been able to develop through reinvestment and working in win/win partnerships. The resulting step changes in education and disease prevention will have tamed the developing world's biggest killers. A side effect for developed nations will be a reduction in the threat of terrorism.

The world will feel more secure. There will be a feeling of brotherhood between nations, people and religions based on tolerance and understanding.

On a personal level, you will have clearer direction, whether it is from the leaders of your country, the organisation you work for or yourself. It will feel as if your input and ideas are valued.

You will have more positive interactions with other people. When disagreements or problems inevitably occur, a greater inner strength and confidence will mean that instead of looking to attribute blame to other parties you will be more able to understand the other viewpoint and find the best solution for all. You will see that those who look to blame, control or judge others lack the self-confidence to take full ownership for their part in a situation, but are doing the best they can.

People from vastly different backgrounds will listen to each other more, take different perspectives on board and then come to significant decisions that offer the best opportunities for the majority in the long term. This approach will have caused a step change in co-operation and therefore will have enabled many breakthroughs in the world.

Your days are likely to be filled with feelings such as joy, fulfilment, happiness, enthusiasm, empowerment and love.

How does this 'new coffee' smell to you?

Does it sound so fanciful that you can't believe it (like the round world we were talking about earlier)? Some people are already living in this world. You can find great examples of these things happening today . . . if you know where to look.

Knowing where you are going is only half the story. You have to know where you are now if you want to be able to understand the differences and plot the route from here to there, so let's have a look at how the world is through the eyes of the current paradigm.

Today's 'Modern World'

On a macro level, the big news stories are shocking. Behind the headlines are the same old problems and accusations. The ability of individuals to understand other people's points of view seems to be very limited. Positions are often entrenched and as a result there are continual cycles of violence and bloodshed in many areas of the world.

The current world stage is dominated by terrorism. The simplified situation seems to be that rich Western governments and organisations operate unfairly in the world. Those who are disadvantaged by their approach feel trapped and no one seems to listen. Eventually things get so bad for some that life seems to be pretty worthless compared to the promises of extremists: 'Anything has to be better than just sitting here enduring this, even suicide.' Invasions and wars inevitably increase the number of people willing to take up the cause. More and more people are killed on both sides. Egos don't back down or admit they were wrong. We seem to be stuck in a vicious cycle.

Vicious cycles create centrifugal forces that force people further and further apart. Individuals from different backgrounds often group together, separating themselves from others. As they confirm with each other how 'right' they are, they lose trust in people 'on the other side' and see them as 'wrong', often demonising them. This is not just limited to global issues, it is a trend in our everyday lives.

An imbalance exists in the world between the 'haves' and the 'have nots'. The gap is widened each year because the 'haves' are in charge and their main concern seems to be to 'have more'. These 'haves' would like to live in a peaceful world, but not if it means they have to make any personal sacrifice. World trade is unequal. Poverty is rife, even though it could be eradicated permanently by some simple measures. We are unconsciously making a choice to keep things as they are.

The world feels like a dangerous place. There seems to be a feeling of tension and mistrust between different nations and religions based on a lack of understanding or acceptance. This has a significant influence on the way the world works – people look out for themselves first.

Mankind's activity in the world is more unsustainable than it has ever been. Despite knowing the potentially dire consequences, the environment is raped on a daily basis for man's use and to generate more wealth for the rich. Biodiversity throughout the world is plummeting. More animals are added to the endangered species list each year. Rainforests are disappearing at an alarming rate each day. Temperatures are increasing and the weather is becoming more extreme. Blah, blah, blah. We know this, we say we care, but we forge on blindly doing the same things. Unconsciously we are choosing this way, even though it may not seem like it to you.

On an individual level, there does not seem to be any great future direction, whether it is from the leaders of the country, organisations or individuals. People seem to vote for the 'best of a bad bunch', rather than a truly inspiring leader. Most companies just seem to exist to make more money next year. It is as if we are all making the most out of things the way they are, whilst waiting for something.

People rarely listen. You may have given up trying to improve things as your views don't seem to be valued. You may feel that alone you can't make a difference, so you might as well join in with the rest and make the most of things now until a groundswell of people seem deeply committed to a different way. Even then you may not trust their motives as there seems to be little trust around in the world right now.

Most people act to further their own needs. Few seem to really care about whether they or other people reach their full potential or not. Antisocial behaviour amongst young people is on the increase. You see behaviour and attitudes that would never have been tolerated a generation ago. You cannot believe that somehow they think that is an acceptable way to behave.

You may have what you need materially, but you may also feel as if something is missing, otherwise you would surely feel much happier. You may have this sneaking suspicion that there is more to life than just this, but you are not sure what it is. No one else seems concerned, so you shrug your shoulders and continue . . . but that nagging suspicion won't go away.

The Choice

'Don't say I can't, say I won't.'
Fritz Perls, founder of Gestalt Theory

So why are we here when we could be there? Well the good news is that it is purely down to the current paradigm about how the world operates. This is good because it implies that all we have to do is take a different approach and things will change significantly for the better. The tough bit is that this paradigm shift is all about the individual and that means you and me. It means taking personal responsibility for changing the way we approach the world and that is going to be tough. Believe me; I am on that journey.

On the one hand, the good news about this is that 'you' are the only thing you are actually in complete control of and it is the impact of individuals like you and me that will either create the new paradigm or maintain the old. On the other hand taking a good hard look at ourselves and then choosing to change the way we operate is perhaps the greatest challenge we will ever take on. No one wants to be wrong.

The ability to choose is a basic human right. Choice is at the root of what it means to be truly free as a human being. Currently in the Western world there is a choice paradox; we have more access to choice than ever before, yet many of us feel trapped. I often coach people who say, 'I'd love to do x, but I can't', and these are often senior businesspeople who clearly have the talent and abilities to choose a different way. I am here to tell you that you do have a choice. Not only that, your choices can create a huge influence in both your life and the wider world of businesses and governments where traditionally individuals have felt helpless.

In my role as a coach I am privileged in that I have conversations with people that they may not have had with anyone else and there is often a common theme to these conversations. There is a groundswell of people who don't want to keep doing things the old way. As more individuals such as you become aware of the One paradigm, more people choose to live up to their true potential.

On a macro level, the more people that do this, the more mankind will live up to its true potential. A potential it is way short of right now. On a micro level, once you start to see the world through the One perspective, everything changes. You don't need to wait for the others to catch up in order to reap the rewards of this fresh approach. They are there for you right now if you really want them.

You are likely to see some incredible changes in these people. These people will make some incredible choices and experience some amazing personal results. You could be one of them. But before you can make the choice, you have to be aware of what you are choosing.

Levels of Awareness

On the surface it seems as if you are either aware of something or you are not. It is a simple 'either or' scenario, but increasingly as I coach people it has become clear that there are four different levels to awareness and it is important to understand these.

Level 0: 'I am unaware of it'

At this level an individual has no awareness of something. This individual does not know an alternative way and it is hard therefore to choose a different way.

Level 1: 'I hear it'

At this level an individual hears of a different way. This is the most basic level of awareness. Just because someone has heard it, does not mean they have seriously considered it or even agree with it. They just know that someone somewhere does things a different way. Some people's backgrounds and approach in life seem to be hardwired to limit awareness to this level. Often this is because they don't want to be seen as having been 'wrong' in the past.

Level 2: 'I know it'

This is an interesting level. At this stage people have heard the alternative, have given it due consideration and have decided internally that they agree with this alternative. On the surface, the change seems to have occurred. It is almost as if the hard work is done, but of course it isn't. Their behaviour has yet to catch up with their awareness. They know it, but they don't do it.

Level 3: 'I live it'

This is where awareness has finally 'bottomed out' and people have made a conscious choice that they are truly living. This is the smoker who says they want to give up and then does it. Their words and their actions are consistent.

As we go through this book, you will realise that you are at different levels of awareness in regard to different elements of the One paradigm. If this book enables you to move up this scale of awareness, it will have achieved its main purpose. It is unlikely that upon finishing this book, you will truly be living all elements consistently at level 3. The journey to the new paradigm is more likely to be a marathon than a sprint.

An interesting exercise at this point is to consider what aspects of your life you are at level 2 awareness of.

- *What do you 'know' (level 2), but not 'live' (level 3)?*
- *What is stopping you from moving to level 3 on this subject?*
- *What step could you take to live it a little more instead of just talking about it?*
- *Once you have taken that step reflect on how hard it was to make that change.*
- *What is it like for you living in level 3 awareness more of the time?*

Authenticity is a key element of unleashing the power of your true potential as we will find out later on. You cannot be truly authentic unless you are living in level 3 awareness.

You Versus the World

The old paradigm is the general approach held by the majority of the world. It is likely to be held by your friends and family. On the surface of it, you may think that there is little you can do to change things for the better – after all you are but one person. Here we have another interesting paradox. 'The world' is only made up of lots of individuals just like you. This is one reason why change can be so hard. Everyone thinks they can't make a difference alone, so no one tries.

People often say 'it's just a drop in the ocean', but what do you think the ocean is made of if it is not drops?

This book will reach many people just like you. It will be the actions of individuals just like you that will change the ocean.

So there are two perspectives to consider as we move through the book:

1 *The Worldwide Perspective*
   This is the ocean that is made up of drops. As we look at different aspects of the One paradigm, consider where the world currently is on the awareness scale. Clearly this varies between countries and regions, but it gives you an idea of where the world is on the journey.

2 *Your Personal Perspective*
   This is the most important one. As you read through the book, consider how your level of awareness changes and what you want to do with that shift. Will you bring the worldwide average up or down?

The world is preparing for a mindset change. You can help with awareness. Often people see this to mean that they should go and do a sales job, 'converting' people, but it is actually much more rewarding and effective to just move up the awareness scale yourself. Children can teach us a lot. If you have children, you will know that they do what you *do*, not what you *say*. Children are only interested in 'level 3' awareness as that is the only one that really counts.

They are right. Quietly taking up level 3 awareness is the most effective way of getting the message out there. You will find out why later in the book.

Mankind's Journey

Mankind is on a journey. Some call it evolution. There is a physical aspect to this. On a long timescale, we evolved from hairy apes that walked on all fours to hairy hominoids, to hominoids that walked upright (*Homo erectus*), to the balder current version of our species – *Homo sapiens*. On a much shorter timescale you can see the differences just in the last few hundred years. For example, we have to crouch to avoid bumping our heads on the beams in old houses because we are much taller on average now that we used to be just a few years ago.

Alongside this there is also an evolution of thinking. The generally held paradigm at any time in history reflects the general stage of evolutionary thinking that mankind has reached. As paradigms have changed through the ages, they have enabled us to take a different perspective on the way the world works. This change has then resulted in dramatic progression and advancement as the different perspective enables breakthroughs that were not possible whilst looking at things through the old paradigm. It unlocks a whole area that we weren't even considering before. Then over time that great new paradigm that initially gave us so much is superseded by the next one. This is the way of the world. Enabling this evolution of thinking is part of our purpose.

You cannot skip paradigms to get to the 'ultimate' one. It may be that there is no such thing anyway. Each paradigm plays an important role in itself and then sets the stage for the next one to supersede it. We could not be preparing for a new paradigm if we did not have all the things that the old world paradigm has brought us. The current old world paradigm is not 'wrong'. It has just advanced us to the stage where we are poised for the next one. In many ways it actually gave birth to the One paradigm. It has done its job.

Your Journey

You are also on a journey. You evolve physically and mentally over the years. You will probably have changed some of your views on things as you have gained more awareness and experience in your life. It's strange. I felt as if I knew it all at 20. Now in my late 30s it is a fact that I know much more than I did then, but I feel as if there is so much more that I don't know. It feels like an exciting journey. My granny is well into her 80s and she still has an innate curiosity that means she is still finding out new things. I hope I'm like her when I'm that age. Life stays interesting no matter how old you are from a perspective of curiosity.

The American psychologist Abraham Maslow published a paper entitled 'A Theory of Human Motivation' in 1943. In this he outlined the 'hierarchy of needs' shown below.[3]

Maslow's theory considers what motivates humans to behave a certain way. He identified five different levels of fundamental human need from the most basic (physiological) right up to the

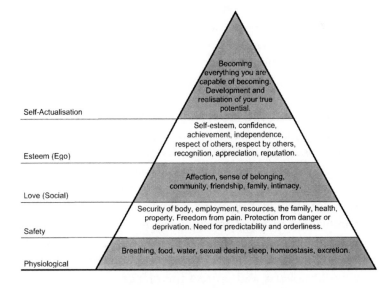

Self-Actualisation — Becoming everything you are capable of becoming. Development and realisation of your true potential.

Esteem (Ego) — Self-esteem, confidence, achievement, independence, respect of others, respect by others, recognition, appreciation, reputation.

Love (Social) — Affection, sense of belonging, community, friendship, family, intimacy.

Safety — Security of body, employment, resources, the family, health, property. Freedom from pain. Protection from danger or deprivation. Need for predictability and orderliness.

Physiological — Breathing, food, water, sexual desire, sleep, homeostasis, excretion.

most advanced (self-actualisation). He suggested that once basic physiological needs have been met, they no longer act as a strong motivator. Factors in the level above then become more compelling. An unmet need is a strong motivating force in human beings.

• *Which level do you think currently motivates you, when considering this pyramid?*

Most people in the developed world are motivated by factors in the esteem level, also known as the 'ego' level. Whilst there will always be some people motivated by factors in the lowest level (physiological) and some by factors in the highest level (self-actualisation), the majority of us operate in this ego space.

Much of my leadership work is focused around these top two levels, but on a recent trip to work with African leaders, the reality of this pyramid was brought into stark focus. Rains had failed in the east of the country and food was scarce. When our physiological needs are not met, we are focused on the bottom level of the pyramid. We see the world from a basic perspective. As I had flown in to the capital, I had seen significant floods where too much rain had fallen too quickly. Here individuals would not have the safety of a roof over their heads, so their view on the world would be influenced strongly by the second level of safety and security.

People who unleash the power of their true potential are motivated by and operate predominantly in the 'self-actualisation' level. The One perspective helps to facilitate the move from ego to self-actualisation. This is the tough journey we have been talking about so far. The awakening of level 3 awareness in us represents the next stage of human evolution.

The global stage is of course merely the ocean that reflects our individual drops. The way the governments of the West interact on the world stage is clearly ego dominated. If it were not, they would be working together harmoniously to end world poverty and protect the planet.

The prevalence of egoic behaviour is reaching an all-time high as individuals in the West experience a higher standard of living than ever before. More and more people are moving up from the social level of belonging into the esteem level and people already in the esteem level are becoming even more ego dominated. The ego level is swelling to epic proportions. In the history of mankind there have never been so many people at this level before. By its nature, the ego level is predominantly self-centred. It is largely this level of thinking that is killing the planet and raising the stakes.

It also means that more people than ever before are poised at the top of the ego level. These are the people who feel on a deep level that despite having more than ever in their life, something is missing. It is these people who will benefit most from increased self-awareness. It is these people who are poised to make a real difference in their own lives by living the One paradigm and ascending to the self-actualisation level. You could be one of these people.

The Change

'You cannot change the world.
Change yourself and you change your world.
Be the change you want to see in the world.'
Gandhi

This book will show you some things that may change your opinion of how the world works. This may enable you to make some big choices, that maybe you would not even have considered before. You may undergo significant change for the better, but the path of change is a tough one.

As a leadership consultant and coach I regularly take people through the process of personal realisation and subsequent change. Initially there is often resistance, fear, lack of confidence or denial – however once a client has taken the first step of accepting the reality and begun to work on the change it becomes easier. Although the journey may be tough at first, things improve and eventually it is as if a great weight has been lifted. On reflection the taking on of great personal challenges results in the most significant personal developments. These are often cited as among the most rewarding things people have ever done.

I believe that the first step in changing something is to understand it and appraise it, but not to linger on it. Where did it come from? Why do we currently do it? What do we get out of it, because let's face it, if we did not get something out of it, we would not do it in the first place, would we? What does it cost us? Once we have done this, we should be in a good position to decide whether we want to change it or not. If we decide we want to change, that is a great first step, but we then need to know what we can practically do differently and what will be in it for us. I believe that if there is nothing in it for us personally in the short, medium and long term, then we will all revert back to the old ways very quickly. The rest of the book will cover all these areas.

For those of you with a nagging suspicion that there must be more to life than this, you are right. The ideas in this book will help you to draw back the curtain. But beware. Once you have opened Pandora's Box, there is no going back. Do you feel ready for the ultimate journey of self-discovery? I'm on it and it's a rough ride; I'll share my story with you as we go. Are you ready to start unleashing the power of your true potential on the world?

The first part of this book explains the three foundations to the One paradigm. Seeing the world through these eyes will help you to open the door to your self-actualisation. The second part makes this perspective personal, offering exercises that *you* can undertake to shed light on the big questions of *your* life. What does *your* true potential look like? What does a truly fulfilling life look like for *you*? Answering these questions is a fundamental part of self-actualising. Answering them allows you to live in line with the One paradigm and ascend to the top of Maslow's hierarchy – the ultimate level of human development.

Strap on your seatbelts – let's go.

The First Foundation of One: Everything is Related

The Age Of Reason

About 300 years ago there was a paradigm shift that brought about the 'Age of Reason'. This was a period during which rationality and logic took over from tradition and superstition. This happened for a reason and it enabled the human race to advance into the modern age, including the industrial revolution that occurred just 200 years ago.

Before the Age of Reason, people had attempted to understand 'the whole' (i.e. life on earth) with overarching religious and superstitious explanations. The 'leaders' of this paradigm were those who practised old school magic and the highest of these developed into the alchemists. Every court in the land had its own alchemist and these became known as magicians. The work of these people was not limited to the light-hearted magic tricks of today. They were knowledgeable in the world and the elements that made it up. They conducted experiments and discovered more. They were the scientists of the day. Where there were gaps in knowledge, superstition, magic and religion filled them in.

The leaders of this paradigm eventually came to the conclusion that the interrelated systems of the world were far too complex to ever be understood fully, but that separate elements could be understood and that would develop awareness. The paradigm changed to one of, 'Forget the whole – you could never understand it. Instead focus on rigorous analysis of the separate bits. Leave no stone unturned. Accept nothing, except things that can be fully explained.'

The Age of Reason caused a huge increase in scientific discovery. Science and reason became the accepted norms, often running roughshod over spiritual beliefs and religions that had played a significant role in the previous world paradigm. Suddenly the world was open to a new interpretation of scientific rigour. Science tends to be binary – it searches to categorise things in black and white. In fact 'separation' and 'categorisation' were key elements of the Age of Reason.

History is littered with examples of where humans have applied 'separate' and 'artificial' solutions to problems and have escalated them rather than solved them due to a lack of appreciation of the whole. Take for example the DDT interventions in the 1960s. To control insects that were pests to farmers an incredibly powerful new pesticide, DDT, was created. It was liberally sprayed everywhere and the insects died. Hooray!

But of course it did not stop there. The animals higher up the interrelated food chain, that ate the insects, continued to eat the dead ones with DDT in them. The more DDT you eat, the more concentrated it becomes in your body; the higher up the food chain you are, the more concentrated DDT becomes in your body. At the top of the farmland food chain back in the 60s were birds of prey. DDT made their eggshells so thin that as they sat on them in the nest, they broke. Their populations crashed. There was a knock-on effect back down the chain. Over time, the result was that the animals that ate farmyard pests were more adversely affected than the insects. Natural balances were upset and the farmers were actually left in a worse position. Oh and by the way, humans are right at the top of the food chain. DDT was thankfully banned before it could significantly affect humans.

Separation and categorisation enabled us to understand more than ever before. It played an important role. But of course nothing actually happens in isolation. Nothing. The systems and processes of the world in which these separated scientific elements or animals act are incredibly complex. You cannot define them in isolation. Knowledge is eventually limited by separation. But on one level separation has been something we have pursued for thousands of years.

Get Me Away From Nature

We (*Homo sapiens*) have been on a quest to separate ourselves from the natural world ever since we first evolved some 120,000 years ago. To some extent it has been the purpose of human life. To appreciate the situation back then, you need to put yourself in your distant ancestors' shoes. Imagine yourself alone and naked in the African bush, but not the African bush of today, one with far greater numbers of wild animals. Imagine the giant sabre-toothed cats of the day, for whom you were preferred prey. Imagine the horror of the night as you heard the screams of another family member dragged off and devoured. Imagine the comfort of being close to the campfire. Is it any wonder that with this heritage we somehow feel more warmth next to an open fire today than the heat alone warrants?

The natural world was wild, unpredictable and dangerous. As we learnt to harness fire and make tools we separated ourselves from nature as much as possible, eradicating or controlling immediate dangers and building fences. We transitioned from hunter-gatherers who were totally at the mercy of nature to growing crops and keeping animals. With farming came an increase in control.

We were so desperate to separate ourselves from nature that we did not limit ourselves to physical fences, we built psychological ones too. The Old Testament cites that God made man on the sixth day to 'rule over all the animals'. We were created on a separate day to the rest of life on earth. We were not part of the rest of life on earth. Finally we were defined as its master by the highest power – God (also often defined as a separate entity). Phew. We wanted to be separate and better than the rest of nature. Now it had to be true.

Ego Neurosis

The struggle of separateness is not limited to us and the natural world – it occurs between cultures, religions and individuals too. Whenever someone is operating in the ego level, there is an inherent part of them that wants to be defined and play out a 'role'. Some quietly want to be seen as better than others. If someone else does something a different way, they often belittle it. The threat of a different way (that could be better) unnerves the ego and it acts to defend itself.

We are currently on a difficult journey because the current 'black and white' world paradigm states that there has to be a 'right' way of doing things. If someone is right, then that means that someone else must be wrong. No one wants to be wrong. If you take a basic assumption that in any difference of opinion someone has to be right and someone has to be wrong, the world suddenly becomes a very competitive place. Egos defend themselves everywhere. This arguing over details can start to take over as the main point to life and I bet you can think of someone you know for whom this is broadly true.

I wonder if people would say it is true of you?

We find that the neurotic desperation for us to be 'separate from' and/or 'better than' other people gets in the way of us achieving our true potential. We are therefore stuck in the ego level.

The Modern World Paradigm: Separateness

So what happens as a result? We act as separate entities in the world and we focus on 'differences' rather than 'similarities'. Your DNA sequences are 98% identical to a chimpanzee's, yet we see ourselves as completely different to them. We are human; they are part of a completely separate animal kingdom. We tend to have a blinkered approach to our impact in the world. We tut-tut at the deforestation of the tropics, yet if we could only take a step back and see how the way we live our lives perpetuates that process, we might be able to do something about it.

But we don't want to be wrong and we would prefer not to change, so we don't look too hard into the details. Somehow if we don't know how we are having a negative impact, then it is OK – we are not to blame. Meanwhile the deforestation continues, the chimpanzees that are 98% the same as you and me die through lack of habitat and we continue on. Unconsciously we tend to either adjust the blinkers so that we do so without regret or we wait to be led by others (who are waiting to be led by us). We are destroying the One web of life that we have. We are killing our relations.

The modern world way focuses on differences so much that we start to think other people are fundamentally different to us in how they operate in the world. We get defensive. We use tactics to forge our way in a world that seems separate, threatening and 'out to get us'. We act in a suboptimal way, because effort is wasted on short-term competitive measures rather than long-term collaborative ones.

We do not collaborate as much as we could because there is a lack of trust. There is a lack of trust because if people are out to get us, we may as well try to get one over on them first. But the more we do this, the more it becomes true, even if it wasn't true in the first place. We often assume the worst when meeting strangers. We create a self-fulfilling prophecy. We live in and perpetuate the old 'separate' paradigm.

So what's the alternative?

Stop the Struggle and Embrace the Inescapable Truth

Think back up your family tree. Think of your mum and dad, your grandparents and beyond. If you went back far enough, your family tree and mine would join up. That is a fact. You and I are related (nice to meet you by the way). You can be black, white, yellow or brown. You can be Christian, Muslim, Hindu or unreligious. You can come from Africa, America, Europe or Asia. You can be a businessman, a housewife, the president or a native tribesman. You can be young, middle-aged or old.

It does not matter.

This is one of the world's inescapable truths.

We are related.

Stop reading for a second and look at the people around you. You are related to them too, no matter how different they seem. How do you think someone would act towards their fellow relations if they truly took on this perspective to life and lived it at 'level 3' awareness every day?

Why not take a moment to write in your notebook:

- *How would you act differently if you saw other people as your relatives?*

But it doesn't stop there. If you subscribe to the widely accepted theory of evolution and you go back beyond the first human that evolved, you also find yourself related to all the apes (our closest living ancestors) too. That is also a scientific fact. Take this to its limits and you share a common ancestry with every reptile, fish, bird and plant that has ever lived, right back to the first spark of life that occurred. Every-thing, and I mean EVERYTHING, came from this initial spark of life.

This is the Oneness of life on earth. We all came from the same spark of life that occurred millions of years ago. This is one of the world's inescapable truths. If you become aware of this at level 3, if you really live it every day, you see the world differently.

Just doing this can be a profound and moving thing.

Stromatolite Appreciation

Scientists suggest that the first life that occurred on the planet was probably a stromatolite. This is a type of blue-green algae that lives in the inter-tidal zone and it can still be seen today in a few remote places. Standing alone on the West Australian coast, I watched the sea splash through some early one morning. I have to admit that at first glance they were pretty uninspiring to look at; just a few slimy green lumps. But consider this: when they first turned up 3.5 billion years ago, there was no oxygen on the planet. Nothing else could live.

These lumps gradually photosynthesised and gave off minute amounts of oxygen. Slowly over millions of years this activity changed the atmosphere's oxygen level, bringing it up to today's average of around 21%. As oxygen increased, more complex life could be supported and things started to happen. Stromatolites evolved into other algae and plankton. Plankton became fish, became amphibians, became reptiles, became mammals, became apes, became humans and now here you are, reading this book.

You owe everything you have and everything you are to those slimy green lumps. They are a part of your personal biological heritage. Your journey into being here today began with them.

Evolution provides us with the first foundation of One: everything is related.

As the sea started to shimmer in the golden light of a new sunrise, I looked upon those slimy lumps with a new-found respect. No matter what we do as a species, it will never touch what this distant relation of ours did. Never. We think we are so clever, but our achievements pale into insignificance when compared to these simple algae. I was humbled by this experience. Because of the tipping point we are at today being humbled by nature has become critical to our survival.

When I say 'our survival', in truth I don't necessarily mean you and me, although some of us will inevitably suffer and die as a result of what we are on the verge of if we don't change. I am referring to the future of the human race at large being able to operate in the world as we know it. I am probably referring to your children. I am certainly referring to your grandchildren.

I invite you to take a good hard look at them next time you see them. Really look deep into their eyes. It may help us to move up the awareness ladder and make some of today's issues such as global warming personal. I think that making it personal is the only way you and I are going to have a chance of saving them from some miserable events in the near future.

So why have we not already made that choice? Why do the global, inclusive relationships of One seem so distant from us? Why does this huge significant truth seem like a pipe dream when our hectic modern lives seem so real and essential? Why do we feel so separate from the power of One?

The One Relation Challenge

The world seems to be at 'level 2' awareness around the fact that everything is related. We 'know it', but don't yet 'live it'. Most people have heard of evolution and subscribe to its theories, but we do not live as if we truly believe it.

With awareness comes 90% of the solution, so let's take a few moments to answer some questions that will help bridge the gap between level 2 and 3 awareness. If you capture your thoughts in your notebook you can start to bring them into reality.

- *What would you and I be doing if we lived in level 3 awareness of the inescapable truth that everything is interrelated?*
- *We know it, why do we not live it?*
- *What gets in the way for you personally?*

Here's a challenge: take a look at the relationships you have
with
1   Your close friends/family.
2   The wider human race: all the people you meet.
3   The 'whole' (i.e. the environment of life on earth).

* *How would you score yourself out of ten for living as a
  truly related being in these relationships?*
* *How do you contribute to the holistic, interrelated web
  of life on this planet?*
* *What one simple thing could you do to increase your
  scores?*
* *Will you do it?*
* *If not, why not?*
* *If so, when do you think you could get round to it?*
* *When you have done it, how did it make you feel?*
* *Where are you on the ladder of awareness?*
* *How could you spend more time at level 3?*

Being Related

What does adopting the inescapable truth that everything is
related look like in real life?

Here's a little example. Recently someone cut me up as I
drove in my car. The other driver slowed me down and
seemed to be deliberately getting in my way. I saw the driver
through 'ego glasses' as separate from me and out to get me.
Eventually I drew level and glared across, expecting to see an
aggressive man gesticulating at me. Instead there was a
young lady who was completely oblivious to the whole situation. I had created an imaginary monster where there was
none. The old world paradigm was alive and well in me.

On reflection, the whole incident was actually about me
being late for an appointment, not about her driving at all.
She had done nothing wrong. I had caused myself stress for
no reason. I had not succeeded in getting to my destination

any quicker, but I had succeeded in making my blood boil. I had increased the likelihood of doing something silly and either crashing the car or being caught for speeding – either of which would have slowed me down much more. I arrived at my meeting in a suboptimal sate. I didn't do a great job. What a waste of effort.

Rather than separateness, a more Oneful approach to this situation would have been to view the other driver as related to me and consider the similarities between us instead of making up differences. Instead of assuming an aggressive, competitive situation, I could have assumed the other driver was actually just like me and only doing what I would do in their situation.

If they were young, they were probably a learner and therefore not a fast driver. I was a learner once; I would have appreciated patience from other drivers as I gained confidence. If they were old, then maybe their reflexes were not as fast as they used to be so they were driving carefully . . . just like my granddad does . . . just like I will one day. If they were middle-aged, maybe they had something on their mind that was distracting them, maybe an ill relation. That was certainly me recently. It doesn't cost anything to assume the best, but it gives you significantly more patience to deal with an issue.

We are all related and our similarities far outweigh our differences in the big scheme of things. It doesn't really matter how you bring this inescapable truth to life – whatever works for you. Is your ego really so underdeveloped that you need to compete in road rage to bolster it? Or are you able to step up and operate at the next level?

If you view the world as interrelated and therefore assume the best in people, you are more likely to interact in the spirit of One. Instead of focusing on what is wrong or wasting your energy on competing with another, you are free to focus your time and energy on your own fulfilment and happiness. This in turn increases the likelihood of you reaching your true potential. This breeds calmness, wisdom and optimal performance. It tends to bring out the best in others. It costs you nothing. With time, even if the driver *is* aggressive, you are able to authentically rise above it. The stresses and strains of modern life gently fall away. You are less likely to become one of those WHO statistics. You are more likely to begin unleashing the power of your true potential.

That was a small example in everyday life that any of us may encounter, but the One perspective works (or not) on the global stage too – it's all just a matter of the number of drops involved. Let's take a look at a big example. How could adopting the One perspective that we are all related have prevented one of the biggest massacres of our time?

The Rwandan Genocide

Bill Clinton cited the massive Rwandan genocide of 1994 as the greatest regret of his presidency. This was a significant event in our recent history, but the separateness that caused it began a hundred years earlier.

The Belgians took control of Rwanda after the First World War and wanted to separate the population out into blue- and white-collar workers. They entered into a series of arbitrary measurements like 'length of nose' and then categorised people as either 'Hutus' or 'Tutsis'. The Tutsis were then randomly chosen to assume positions of power. The Hutus were treated like second-class citizens by them, even though the similarities between Hutus and Tutsis far outweighed the illogical differences that the Belgians had decided to single out.

In 1959 the Hutus took over control and reversed the situation, banishing the Tutsis to menial tasks. The bitterness from the Hutus over the way they had been treated simmered over the years and finally boiled over in 1994. Despite warnings and horrifying television footage coming out of the country immediately, the world was slow to react.

Most people had never heard of Rwanda and took the 'separateness' point of view that it was a long way away and there was nothing they could do. If it was important, it was assumed that the world's governments would pick it up and do the right thing. They didn't, and a few weeks later over a million innocent men, women and children had been hacked to death with machetes.

So how could things have turned out differently if any party at any stage had adopted the One perspective that we are related rather than the old world view that we are separate? The Belgians could have avoided the whole situation by treating the population as a whole instead of making up differences and categorising people. When the Tutsis were put in power, they could have chosen to focus on the similarities between themselves and their fellow Rwandans (now called Hutus), treating them with respect rather than abusing the power they were given. When the Belgians left, the Hutus took over and they could have done the same, putting emphasis on the independence of the country from colonial rule and the re-uniting of its population above any old problems.

They could have literally buried the hatchet there and then.

But it doesn't stop there. The relations and connections of the Oneness of life transcend international boundaries (another way of separating people). International governments adopting the One perspective could have dismissed the facts that separated Rwanda from their countries and acted decisively to avert the crisis. Beyond that there was also a more personal possibility. Instead of focusing on the fact that we had never heard of Rwanda, Western people like us could have focused on the similarities; that families just like ours were in the process of being slaughtered in their homes. We could have made a noise that our governments could not ignore and could have encouraged more decisive action on the world stage. That would have been the power of One; a million innocent people saved.

But no one focussed on the One perspective. Separateness prevailed. A million innocent people (just like you and me) were condemned to a month of terror, rape and murder.

It is hard to imagine what it must have been like. If you get a chance to see the film *Hotel Rwanda*, it will give you an idea. I watched it with a group of Tanzanian government officials. Tanzania is the neighbouring country where the post-genocide trials were held. Despite it being more than a decade ago, the wounds and memories ran deep and many wept. The closer you are to people, the more the power of One seems tangible. The easier it is to really feel the relationship. Perhaps the most documented example is through twins that once shared the same womb being able to experience what the other is feeling at certain times. Have you ever phoned a loved one just as they were picking up the phone to you? It's the same kind of thing.

Separation has enabled us to understand things a lot more clearly, but the time has come to re-establish a more balanced view. We need to start viewing the world through more holistic glasses. Actually the *relationships* between the elements of the whole are more important than the individual elements themselves. We have finally reached a point in our species' evolution where we can start to appreciate the whole, but only if we view the world through different glasses; the glasses that say 'Everything is related'. From this perspective, life is also more positive and enjoyable. It's not a hardship, it doesn't cost you anything, it's just about breaking an old habit and forming a new one.

Take some time to personally embed this part of the One perspective. As you live it, seek out the evidence to make it true for you and embrace it at level 3 awareness. This may present a significant personal challenge, especially with today's hectic modern lifestyles, but it is important to create a firm foundation of this cornerstone before exploring the next.

The second foundation of the One paradigm presents us with an even more shocking truth.

Everything is connected.

The Second Foundation of One: Everything is Connected

What do you know about quantum physics?

Not much? Me neither.

As I began my personal journey of discovering One, I became aware that something was missing from the standardised view we have of the world and our place within it. The basic fundamental cornerstones of scientific proof, rational thought and definitions of how the world works were somehow incomplete. I could sense something else around the edges; something that on the one hand was fundamentally different and profound, yet at the same time was remarkably subtle and elusive. As I researched this book I came across quantum physics and suddenly everything fell into place.

In a nutshell it is a relatively new field of study and is a branch of physics that studies the behaviour of extremely small particles. What quantum physicists have discovered is that when you get down to the very smallest particles, the very building blocks of everything else, they behave in a funny way. At this fundamental level of matter, particles do not behave as we would expect them to under the normal 'laws' of physics.

As you can imagine, this has created hot debates in scientific circles. Quantum physics represents a new paradigm of thought in this arena and as a result many of the old leaders have found it hard to accept. At the moment it is seen as a 'niche'. I suspect that at some stage in the future it will become more mainstream and many traditional scientific 'laws' will be overturned or modified as a result of its impact. As we speak I know of people who are making breakthroughs by applying a quantum physics approach instead of the traditional approach in their chosen disciplines.

Magicians and alchemists gave birth to the present-day scientific paradigm. How apt that cutting-edge physics, one of the great disciplines of the age of reason, should then reach its peak by discovering something that has the potential to destroy the previous few hundred years of its own 'laws'. How amazing that in the process it gives us a reference that may actually fill some of the gaps that superstition and religion filled in the past. As I said before, each paradigm gives birth to the next.

The Connection

In 1982 the Aspect Experiment was undertaken in France.[4] This involved splitting two quantum (i.e. very small) particles and isolating them from each other, with a huge distance between them. When one was rotated clockwise, the other did the same. When the rotation was reversed, the other copied. There were no apparent links between the particles. Nothing we have proved in traditional physics can explain how this happens. The old world paradigm does not have the capacity to explain this.

So here is the situation:

1   *It is a scientific fact that it happens.*
2   *We can't fully explain it yet.*
3   *It has the potential to overturn previously held beliefs about how the world works, so people are reluctant to accept it.*

So what do we do with that?

In this day and age, it is very difficult to overturn something if you can't fully explain it. The modern world view is that you always have to know why. We live in a time where we feel as if everything has been discovered and there is no more mystery in the world. Here's an interesting paradox though – in other, more established, areas of physics we often don't know why things happen either. We just don't question them because they are 'established'. They are part of the old paradigm, so we accept them as fact.

For example, we have a current understanding that 'gravity' is an attraction between two objects. The bigger the object and the closer you are to it, the more power behind the pull. The earth is massive and you are very close to it, so you are strongly attracted to it. No matter how hard you jump, you cannot leave its gravitational pull. However, travel far enough away (for example up in space) and the pull is diminished. The moon is much smaller, and when you watch astronauts walking around on it, you can see how much lighter the pull of the moon is compared to the earth because of the size difference.

We all know gravity exists, but guess what? We don't know why! No one has yet come up with a clear theory that explains *why* big objects attract each other. Yet we accept it (and use it) every day. It just happens. Incidentally quantum physics has a theory that offers an explanation of gravity that may one day be proved.

It turns out that we are living in a world based at a certain level on assumptions, even regarding things as fundamental as gravity! Like the child who keeps asking, 'Why?' we eventually run out of answers and say, 'It just does'. If that is the case (and if you are up for it), there is no harm in investigating a different set of answers that link together just as plausibly. This is the different approach that makes up the second cornerstone of the One perspective: that everything is connected. You then just have to decide which paradigm you prefer and gather the personal evidence you need to prove it to yourself.

Why do you think there is there so much resistance to the findings of quantum physics? People don't like change at the best of times, let alone a change that means we have to substantially rewrite the record books. The status quo (or old paradigm) is threatened. Many people's reputations have been built on work they have done based on the old rules. The people who were 'best' at the old rules are likely to be in the positions of most power and influence. They are likely to want to preserve their position. Many of them may feel it is too late for them to change and embrace a new way. As a result, many have reacted defensively to the theories and rational implications of quantum physics.

It is exactly the same with the One paradigm. Many people resist it. They are likely to be people trapped in the ego level with no desire to develop into the self-actualisation level, the pinnacle of human existence. They are likely to be well served by the modern world paradigm and therefore experience little desire to develop any further to fulfil their true potential. They are likely to be comfortable in life and therefore not have the hunger to make a difficult voyage of self-discovery and awareness.

Are you one of them?

The Zero Point Field

The implication of quantum physics is that when you separate things that were once connected, a subtle bond of energy remains between them that we don't fully understand. Not only this, but communication is possible between them. Somehow the particles tested in France 'knew' what was happening to each other and were able to copy. By the way, you are made up of billions of these particles.

We have already established the first foundation of One: that everything is related. All life evolved from the same origin. Everything came from that first spark. Cells subdivided and separated, but they had always once been joined together. Different species evolved, but they always shared the same heritage. Your relations had babies that eventually led to the birth of you and me and even though we may never have met, we still share a common ancestry. We all came from the same place. We were all once joined. Just like the separation in the Aspect Experiment, although you may appear physically separate from others, you and the particles you are made up of share a connection with every living thing. It is just logical.

A subtle web of energy connects us all. As individuals we all make up a part of this energy web. You hold a unique place within it. We are all part of One buzzing energy field. This is profound. You may be unaware of it, but on a subtle level you are communicating with every living thing, and everything around you is communicating with you. The Aspect Experiment proved this.

'Preposterous!' you might well say at this point. 'If there was that much energy buzzing around, we would have been able to detect it years ago and if we couldn't, it would not be worth bothering with anyway!' You would of course be correct. Actually we have been able to detect it for years ... we just didn't know what it was.

For years, sensitive experiments in physics have made a subtraction at the end to allow for this background 'buzz' of energy that was always present. It became known as the 'zero point field'. Oh how things have moved on. The slightly annoying background noise that had to be subtracted to get a 'perfect result' has ended up being a field of study in its own right that threatens to overturn our neatly compartmentalised view of a separate world of 'things'.

The modern world paradigm says, 'The most important element of things is the *matter* they are made up of. Everything is separate and unconnected'.

The One perspective says, 'The most important element of things is the *energy* they are made up of. Everything is interconnected by this energy.'

You are a Radio

Further quantum experiments proved that everything sends out and receives energy, just like a radio transmitter transmits signals and a receiver picks them up. We accept that radios do this, but it turns out that everything does on a subtle level; every particle. That includes you and me. You are made up of particles. You are transmitting and receiving signals as you speak. So am I. So is everything around you. Cool, eh?

Imagine if you could tune into it and pick up messages from the zero point field. Imagine what that would enable you to do. In fact don't imagine. Have you ever walked into a room where you could 'cut the atmosphere with a knife'? Have you ever picked up that someone is upset or angry even before they have said anything? Where do you think that feeling comes from? I believe it is us being able to pick up on the signals that are in the room. If you have felt this, then you have already experienced a little taster of what the zero point field has to offer. This is the essence of the power of One.

Do you know someone who picks up on a situation quickly and invariably seems to be able to take the most appropriate approach, even if it is different each time? Could it be that they are good at receiving information from the zero point field and acting on it, even if they are unaware that is what they are doing?

The field is subtle. So subtle you could easily miss it. It is an integral part of you. It is within you, within others and between everything. It is everywhere. It is omnipresent. On the one hand this is hugely significant. On another level, it has always been there and it always will be, so there is nothing new. Silence is filled with it. You can't 'hear' it in the traditional sense, but you can increase your skill in receiving information from it.

In the second half of this book we will do just that. Often the success (or not) of people's lives depends on tiny differences in timing or choice. Even if you could make a 1% difference to your odds in life, it would help you along the way and give you an advantage. We will look at real tactical ways in which you can develop your ability to extract information from the zero point field.

Modern World Interference

You may be thinking, 'If this zero point field is so important, *why* can't I hear it?' The answer is:

1 *Generally, we are not very good at listening – we will look at ways in which you can develop this skill later.*
2 *The zero point field seems to be 'heard' more easily by individuals in the self-actualisation apex. Most of us are below that in the ego level. We will look at some ways in which you can move towards the apex later.*
3 *This information exists in the silence, in the space between things in a subtle, intangible way. Most of us live in a fast-paced, busy, material world where we are simply not in a position to hear or notice it. The current modern world paradigm gets in the way.*

The modern world is loud, brash, busy and hectic. The current paradigm encourages people to do, do, do. Quiet time has become 'dead' time. Technological advances seem intent on stripping out any 'dead' time. From mobile phones to iPods, we can now 'do' something every minute of our waking day. We 'do' more and more. There is very little quiet time left any more.

This means two things. Firstly, in many ways, people are under more stress now than they have been at any time in our previous history. Like the boiling frogs, we fill our days with more and more stuff because everyone else is doing the same. That scary WHO statistic lies waiting at the end of this road. Somebody said that we are human beings, not human doings. They are right. This level of constant stimulus is not natural and therefore there is a danger it will make us ill.

Secondly, the more we do, the less chance we have to stop and listen; listen to other people on a level where we can sense the quantum energy behind their words; listen to the important messages that lie waiting for us in the zero point field.

If you want to read a more detailed history of the scientific evidence behind quantum physics and the zero point field, in an easy to understand text, then I recommend you read Lynne McTaggart's book *The Field*.[5]

One Connection Challenge

The view that everything is related and interconnected is fundamental to One. This is a significant departure from our traditional way of viewing the world as inanimate separate objects. Stop reading this book for a moment and look around you. Let's take a few minutes out to stop doing and just 'be' for a while.

Take some time to really absorb the people, sights, sounds and smells. All of what you see evolved from that first tiny speck of life. It has a lot to answer for doesn't it? Listen to how people are interacting with each other. Notice the details of the environment you are in and imagine it all linked by that common ancestry. Wooden chairs used to be trees; woollen carpets came from sheep and cotton clothes from plants. They are all connected by the zero point field.

What does it feel like when you *really* own your place in the interrelated web of life on the planet? What does it feel like when you immerse yourself in this breathing, pulsating energy of life that buzzes with activity around the clock? Instead of seeing the world around you as dangerous, separate and out to get you, view it as benign, interrelated and helpful.

Everything came from one speck of life. Everything shares a common ancestry. All the particles that make up everything are quietly communicating with each other. The particles that make up you are communicating with them too. From this higher perspective, the fundamental links, relationships and similarities between things far outnumber the smaller superficial differences.

- *What changes for you when you take on this perspective?*
- *What message is here for you?*

I challenge you to live it for a day. Each time you interact with someone or have a choice to make, do it in the spirit of everything being connected. If you are keeping a notebook as suggested at the beginning, capture what happens.

- *How well did you maintain the perspective that everything is related and connected over the period of a day?*
- *When did you forget and what can you do about that?*
- *What changed for you?*
- *What were the advantages?*
- *Were there any disadvantages for you?*
- *On balance if you enjoyed it, will you live in it again tomorrow?*

We share a common heritage that we cannot escape from. We are all part of the same whole. Everything is subtly interconnected. This is the essence of One. Everything else comes from this. *Everything*.

If you live and act in line with the One perspective, it enables you to tap into a different source of power; a power of incredible magnitude and peace. If we each approached our world from the One perspective, all of the world's problems and difficulties would be solved. Yes all of them. We are now finally at a point in our history where we have the tools and technology at our disposal to begin to take this view and make this world real. We have the resources. The knowledge is out there. Some of us may be a little fuzzy on awareness of what One is and how it works, but spreading awareness of that is the main purpose of this book.

All we actually need to do then is make the choice.

The Third Foundation of One: Nature is the Greatest Power

The modern world way is to approach things from a perspective of separateness, i.e. humankind is separate from the natural world. This has resulted in us seeking artificial solutions to problems. The more humankind has advanced, the more we in the Western world have enjoyed a higher standard of living, but the more removed we have also become from the natural world and what it means to be a member of the human species. In many ways we have created a separate and artificial world for ourselves.

There is nothing inherently wrong with development per se. In fact you could argue that if we were not at the stage of comparative luxury we are now, then there would not be such a groundswell of people in the Western world looking for more out of life – people would be stuck lower down Maslow's hierarchy. The problem is that the artificial world we are living in now has become increasingly out of balance with how we have lived our lives for centuries and this is causing us stress as a species. It is the modern world way of living that is creating the WHO prediction.

The third foundation of the One paradigm is that nature is the greatest power. Rather than separating ourselves even further from nature and making our lives even more artificial, to reach our full potential we need to redress the balance. We actually need to get closer to nature, respect it and tap into its inherent power. For people reaching the self-actualisation level this creates a much deeper and perennial experience of happiness. It also invokes greater reward from less effort.

'Nature' is important on three levels and all have significant relevance for us:

1 *There is what happens naturally in the world: 'nature'.*
2 *There is what comes naturally to us as a species: 'human nature'.*
3 *There is what comes naturally to you as an individual: 'personal nature'.*

Immersing yourself in third-level awareness of all of these is vital to unlocking the power of your true potential. The bigger the gap is between the way you live your life and these three elements, the more stressful life is for you as an individual member of a naturally occurring species on this planet. That's just the way nature works. It's the same for every animal on the planet. It is an inescapable truth. You can fight it and create stress or you can accept it and align yourself with it, making life naturally easier, more abundant and more rewarding.

We have become so far removed from the natural world that vast numbers of people in the West operate in almost entirely artificial surroundings and so they have little connection with or respect for their natural heritage. In many places, especially cities, people can become cut off completely from their natural roots. We have to understand the extent to which we are living artificially, to be aware of what it gives us and what it costs us.

To be able to understand just how important the natural world is to us and just how far away from it we have become, it is useful to gain a perspective on time. As you will come to expect with One, this means the ultimate big picture perspective. It means a perspective that takes in all the time that there has been life on this planet. It means understanding where we as a species fit in to that and ultimately where your life as an individual fits in to the whole.

The Natural World: Perspective on Time

I don't know about you, but I find the multiples of thousands and millions of years that accompany the history of our planet a bit difficult to get my head round. I hear the big numbers, but I can't really grasp what they mean. What counts as recent and what counts as ancient? What are the messages for us behind the facts?

When I was in school I remember someone relating life on the earth to a 24-hour clock. Then I really got it. So let's use that analogy to look at our origins as it brings into stark reality some of the reasons why the WHO predicts we are on the verge of a huge increase in personal stress and depression.

Homo sapiens (that's us) has been around on the earth for 120,000 years. That sounds like a long time until you consider that life on earth has been around for 550 million years. If we take the 24-hour day as a metaphor for the 550 million years that life has been on the planet, then the first spark of life appeared on the dot of 12 midnight. Those stromatolites that we were talking about earlier were doing their thing for a quite a while before anything else appeared.

At quarter past eight in the morning, more complex life forms, like molluscs, developed and just after lunch animals with backbones (vertebrates) arrived. Reptiles evolved after the end of your working day with dinosaurs and coniferous pine trees turning up about half past six. At ten to ten in the evening the first mammal walked on the planet, but it wasn't until ten to midnight that the first hominoid (anthropoid ape related to man) graced us with his presence.

Homo erectus first walked upright at five to midnight and *Homo sapiens* (our species) only just made it through the door at 20 seconds to midnight. The first farming ever took place at 2 seconds to midnight. Christ was born at 0.3 seconds to midnight. The industrial revolution occurred at

0.03 seconds to midnight. The personal computer was entering people's homes at 0.005 seconds to midnight and the internet became accessible at 0.002 seconds to midnight.

Wow. When I first looked at the evolutionary history of our planet from this point of view it gave me a different perspective on what was important in life. Not just 'life' as it applied to my short existence, but 'life' in general. 'Life' has gone about its business by certain natural cycles and patterns over millions of years. Knowing these natural rules and playing in alignment with them makes you better at the game. It seems in many ways as though we have not just lost sight of the natural guidelines that are inherent in the world around us, but we have started to lose sight of the whole game.

We need to appreciate just how out of balance we are with nature. If we don't, there is no compelling reason to change. It would be a shame if we walked off the edge of a cliff and no one had told us it was there, so let's consider how close we are to the precipice. We have been hearing from scientists and conservationists for years that the environment is in danger, but because the life we lead in the West is so artificial, we are removed from it and so we are slow to notice. Here are some thoughts for you to set the scene of how we are poised with respect to nature, the greatest power right now.

The Culmination of World Population

The world's human population has roughly increased as follows:

- *1800: 1 billion*
- *1950: 2.5 billion*
- *2009: 7 billion*
- *2050: 9 billion[6]*

This is a sequence of numbers that draws attention to the importance of our time. Many people alive today will own a unique place in history – they will be the only people ever to witness the tripling of the world's human population. No one else in the history of mankind, past or future, will ever witness this.

I was clearing out the loft yesterday and I found my wife's geography exercise book from school. On 16th September 1983 she wrote, 'The world's population is now over 4,000,000,000'. Just in the time between her writing that and now, we have added the equivalent of the whole world's population in 1800, three times! There was something about seeing her handwriting that brought this home for me. We are in it, now. This is not a removed fact in a dusty text book. This is in our own handwriting. It is personal, real and right now.

We will be the ones who decide how we go about tripling the world's population. It will be part of our legacy and will be talked about in schools for millennia to come.

You cannot triple the world's population and continue to use unsustainable practices without expecting some kind of disastrous payback in the future. The big questions for the sceptic are 'How long can we get away with it?' and 'How close are we to the limit?' Both are incredibly important questions, but also incredibly difficult to answer for sure. Sceptics often use this as an excuse to do nothing.

Are you a sceptic?

The Culmination of the Modern World Lifestyle

'If we follow the same pattern of lifestyle of the US citizen, we need five planets.'
Ahmed Djoghlaf, *Planet Earth: The Future*[7]

The rest of the world looks at America as the role model – they aspire to live that lifestyle. Many of the less developed countries of the world (especially China) are currently undergoing rapid development. The Western world preaches to the poor nations to protect their rainforests, but the Western world cut theirs down years ago as an integral part of their development. Europe used to be completely covered in forest; now forest only represents about 5% of its area.

We only have one earth. All countries cannot develop in the same unsustainable way that we in the West did. Everyone simply can't live the same way as the Americans do now. It is not physically possible. This is an inescapable truth. We don't have five worlds to use up. Currently the modern world paradigm is not taking a viable alternative seriously, because it is more interested in short-term profit than long-term sustainability.

It is an interesting reflection on our time that 'sustainability' is often seen as some kind of optional extra; an inconvenient ideal to strive towards if individuals, organisations and governments are forced to. If something is not sustainable, then its natural equation does not work over the long term. If we don't individually change our approach the unsustainable nature of what we are doing *will* cause ramifications. That is an inescapable truth. If we don't change, something drastic will happen.

The ideal of living the American dream is actually a double-edged sword. Living a lifestyle that is this far out of balance with our natural heritage has negative psychological ramifications on us as a naturally occurring species. Here are some medical facts that demonstrate the personal cost of living the modern world lifestyle at its most extreme.

- *In any given one-year period, 9.5% of the population (about 20.9 million American adults) have a mood disorder.*
- *18.1% of Americans over 18 years old (40 million) have anxiety disorders.*
- *An estimated 26.2% of Americans aged 18 and older (that's about one in four adults) suffer from a diagnosable mental disorder in a given year.*

- *Major Depressive Disorder is the leading cause of disability in the U.S. for ages 15–44.*[8]

So why are other people in the world hankering after this kind of 'luxury' modern lifestyle that costs us so much financially and emotionally? I have met many unhappy businesspeople who have plenty of material wealth and many happy people in developing countries with nothing but a couple of chickens. Wouldn't they be best maintaining the simple but happier lives they have now? What is it that drives people towards this dubious goal?

Ask yourself the question. Why do you do it?

We Are in the Middle of One of the World's Mass Extinctions

'We used to have 1,000 species go extinct every year. Now we are maybe losing between 15,000 and 60,000 species a year. When we discover a new species it is a newspaper headline because it's something exceptional. But the rate of extinction is not exceptional – it's not in the newspapers – because its business as usual.'
E. O. Wilson, *Planet Earth: The Future*[9]

Fossil records show that there have been five mass extinctions in the world's history. They are thought to have been due to significant and incredibly violent events such as massive meteorite hits or enormous volcanic eruptions. To give you an idea of how common they are, the last one saw off the dinosaurs.

We are in the middle of the sixth mass extinction now.

How is this significant world event for you? Do you notice the flames and destruction? It may not seem violent or significant. You may not even know it is happening. That is because this one is unique. It is the first one that has been caused by a species already on the planet. I'm afraid it is down to us. The way our species lives (especially the global knock-on effects of the way we live in the Western world) is now officially classed as one of the six most destructive events in the entire history of our planet.

The scary bit is that we haven't finished yet.

Separateness is the root cause of this. We don't notice the ramifications because we are separate from them. We enjoy the fruits, we play a role in the issues, but we don't see the disastrous knock-on effects that our way of living has because they occur elsewhere. Also we have not crossed the 'tipping point' where things become really serious; more serious even than the world's sixth mass extinction!

The robustness of ecosystems is due in a large part to biodiversity and variety. As you reduce variety, you make the ecosystem less robust. When you reach a 'tipping point', too much is lost, interconnections between species collapse and extinction accelerates massively due to the knock-on effect.

If we wait until we cross this significant tipping point, then we will notice because it will trigger a catastrophic natural disaster. If the past is anything to go by then this will trigger a human catastrophe such as famine or significant conflict over a lack of natural resources. If we wait until then, it will be too late to redress the balance. We have a choice to make. In the future, fossil records will show what we have done. In the future, when we are all dead and buried, the earth's sixth mass extinction will already represent a significant part of our legacy, but we can choose how bad we let it get. Proactivity has never been so important.

The Natural Choice

One of the key reasons we drag our feet in preserving the quality of our planet is that it seems as if the only way we can do it is to make sacrifices and our egos don't want to do that. Abstinence does not work; we can't go back to living in caves.

However, continuing to 'develop' as a human race in an unsustainable way does not work either. We therefore must move in a new direction if we are to evolve towards our true potential as a species.

The first step towards redressing the balance and invoking the sustainable power of nature instead of destroying it, is to understand some of the world's natural systems and processes. If you can then bring these systems to life and live them at level 3 awareness you will be able to bring nature, the world's greatest power, to bear on your life. Life becomes easier, more effective and more fulfilling. Rather than achieving less, you can achieve more. Rather than diminishing your happiness, it increases.

We see natural cycles and processes physically in nature and psychologically within ourselves. They live in parables, sayings and legends. Of course they do; everything is related. They are all different expressions of One. The ways of nature are profound. They are how our world works, physically, mentally and emotionally. Instead of fighting nature's way, we can instead choose to accept it and live more Onefully. Let it all wash over you and go with the flow. Start to work with it and you may be surprised at what it unleashes within you.

Let's look at some of the elements of nature's way. Bringing these to life will increase your awareness and use of nature – the greatest power. They will strengthen the foundations on which you stand as you take on mankind's greatest journey in the next section of this book.

Evolution

Take a look around you. Everything you see is down to evolution. Evolution created everything from the wooden table you sit at to the people around you. The natural rule that causes evolution is actually very simple: every now and then, try something new; make a 'mistake'. If the 'mistake' does not suit its environment, then in the big scheme of things nothing much is lost. If it is better suited to its environment, it sticks. Eventually completely new species can be born this way. You don't come up with a human unless you are prepared to get a monkey wrong every now and then and look at the power that unleashed.

So when was the last time someone you know encouraged evolution; a natural process and incidentally the most powerful force in the world? When was the last time someone at work said to you, 'Hey I trust you – just try something different and if it ends up being a mistake it doesn't matter – we'll learn from it and try something else'? In many organisations, fear of making a mistake has driven people away from trying something new. Instead people focus on repeatedly doing the same thing, even if it is suboptimal. In the event of a mistake, the focus shifts quickly towards finding someone to blame. This stifles evolution, the greatest power on the planet. The result of this kind of approach is that we continue to shuffle along in the same unsustainable direction and increase stress levels in the process.

It is natural to try something new and make mistakes. As Thomas Edison said whilst inventing the light bulb, 'I have not failed. I've just found 10,000 ways that won't work.'

- *When was the last time you tried something new and made a mistake?*
- *Think of a relatively risk-free aspect of your life that is currently not working (for example this could be a small project at work or how you spend your time at the weekends). What would be some different ways of approaching your chosen issue?*
- *Think of at least 10 things you could do differently. Don't worry if you think they would be a mistake for now, just have fun and write down anything – the more outrageous the better.*

When you have finished, consider your list.

- *What new approach will you try?*
- *When will you do it?*

If it goes well, then great – you have successfully applied evolution, the world's most powerful force, to improve something. If it doesn't work, then learn from it and apply the learnings next time you are in the same situation. Either way you have learned from the experience and evolved. Your evolution increases your chance of success next time.

Balance

Nature seeks balance. For example when a species with finite resources undergoes sudden and rapid growth it becomes out of balance with its environment. Natural processes and cycles work to rebalance the situation. A deadly communicable disease may spread quickly through the densely packed population and rebalance its numbers. Conditions may get so overcrowded, stressed and under-resourced that a conflict kills off a significant portion of the population. Whatever it is, something pretty unpleasant takes place if the situation remains out of balance for too long. It is nature's way.

Businesses focus on monetary *growth*. Economies are based on monetary *growth*. However, everything in nature reaches some kind of *balance* in maturity. The only thing that carries on growing ad infinitum in the natural world is cancerous cells. They eventually grow so much that they interfere with their host's natural living systems and eventually kill it. Cancer is unsustainable. The modern world's fiscal and business models are currently based on a similar approach.

We need to learn the importance of 'balance' over 'growth' before it is too late. If we don't, we will continue to take out an overdraft on our planet. Nature is the greatest power.

Nature will find a balance. If we push it too hard it will have to topple physically, financially or psychologically to re-establish some stability. We have just witnessed one of the world's most significant financial meltdowns in the form of the 2008 credit crunch. This is an example of a balancing force triggered by unsustainable growth.

Perpetual growth will not last forever. The time is coming for us to mature. It is time to find some balance.

How balanced is your life? Consider things like the time you spend at work, with family/friends, doing the things you love to do, keeping fit, spending time in nature etc. Add any other aspects that are important to you and give them all a score out of ten for how well balanced they are in the context of your life.

- *Where do you spend too much time?*
- *Where do you spend too little time?*
- *What could you do to redress the balance?*
- *When you have done this, consider its impact on your wellbeing.*

On a macro level, what can you do proactively to help us live in a way that is more in balance with nature (e.g. reducing consumption of the earth's finite resources, reusing something you already have or recycling more of your waste)? Don't do it because you have to, do it because you want to. Do it because it is a natural thing to do. Notice the impact it has on you.

Life's Dice

Stuff happens in life. To a certain extent, everything is down to chance. You roll life's dice each day. Everyone does. For example if you smoke, you roll a certain sided dice to see if you will develop lung cancer. The more you smoke, the fewer the number of sides on the dice and therefore the higher the chance you will roll a '1' and get cancer. If this happens, you start to roll one of life's other dice, the one to see whether you will die from it or not. Don't smoke at all and you add sides to your dice. Getting lung cancer by rolling a '1' is less likely. It can still happen though. That's just the way life works. There's nothing you can do about it. It's not about what's fair and what's not, it is about the way nature works. We signed up to these natural laws when we were born.

Very little in life is guaranteed. However, we can make choices that give us a better chance of rolling the kind of dice numbers that we want. Some things will come off, some things won't. People who unleash the power of their true potential are aware of the dice they roll. They make conscious choices to roll dice that are in line with what they want to get from life. This gives them a much higher probability of leading the life that makes them happy and fulfilled; it is the natural way.

Many people are unaware that they are even rolling dice. Some are rolling the dice that someone else has given them. If they aren't your dice, then who put them in your hand? Your parents? Your partner? The board of your company? Your boss? Who is choosing the dice you are throwing in your life? It is your life, not theirs. You are the only person who can choose to put some dice down and pick up a different set. Not only can you influence the number of sides on your dice, but you can load the roll too. You will learn how to load your dice in the next section of the book.

It is natural to consciously choose the dice that you want to roll in life, to accept the result and then to focus on the next roll. Life's dice are all about probability. There is very little in life that you cannot influence in some way by choosing your dice.

Consider something you would love to have more of in your life (for example love, health, happiness, friends, confidence etc.). What could you do differently tomorrow to increase the probability of more of it turning up? Take that action and notice how the different roll of the dice affects things. The more you roll that dice, the more probability you stand of getting the result you desire. Note the results over time in your notebook.

The Universal Law of Attraction

You naturally tend to attract what you focus on. For example I went to visit my in-laws to see an uncle who was staying with them. The uncle had a reputation for breaking things and I could sense a tense atmosphere in the zero point field as soon as I entered the house. Someone in the room was resonating very strongly, 'Something's going to get broken'.

I felt uncomfortable in the atmosphere so I started playing a silly game with my son, which involved me sitting in a chair whilst lifting him up in the air above me. I had never played this game before. The atmosphere encouraged me to do it. Suddenly there was a loud crack as one of the legs on my chair snapped under the weight of me and my son leaning back in it. 'Something's going to get broken' came true (it was just not the person they thought was going to break something!). It was a self-fulfilling prophecy.

The universal law of attraction is a natural law that states that you attract what you deeply resonate. Someone resonated, 'Something's going to get broken' and it did. Can we put the blame entirely at their door? I don't think so; after all I broke the chair. But did they load life's dice that day? Yes, I think they did. Remember to notice coincidences. 'What a coincidence that the only time you have broken a chair in that house was on the day the clumsy uncle visited.' No coincidence in my mind, merely reinforcement of how this natural law works in conjunction with the zero point field.

Two things are vitally important to understand about the universal law of attraction. Firstly, your subconscious doesn't do negatives. For example, if I say, 'Don't think of a blue banana' it puts the very idea of a blue banana in your head. It could have been that a blue banana could not have been further from your mind and now it's been mentioned, it keeps popping into your mind. Psychologically speaking, your mind has to go to the blue banana first before it can then attempt to remove it. The problem is that even if you could remove it you would be left with a hole in the shape of a blue banana. Even if you focus on something else to fill it, the deeper, underlying reason behind it is to get rid of the blue banana.

'Why are you thinking of purple strawberries?'

'I'm trying to keep that blue banana out of my head ...'

There is no point resonating, 'I don't want any more money issues' because 'more money issues' is the equivalent of the blue banana. You may therefore subconsciously load your dice to somehow attract money issues into your life. Is there something negative that seems to recur in your life over and over again? Is it something you consciously don't want? It could be that focusing on not wanting it keeps attracting it. Don't focus on what you don't want; focus on what you do want instead. For example instead of focusing on *not wanting* money issues, focus on *having* wealth and financial freedom.

Another good example is the kind of partners we attract into our life. At a deep level, we are resonating and focusing on the qualities that continue to show up. We will look at this more in Part 2.

When your actions are consistent with your words and your deeply held beliefs, then you get to throw a dice with better odds *and* load it in your favour. Then you start to live in level 3 awareness of what you are doing. Then you start to unleash the power of your true potential.

It is natural for you to receive what you focus on at a deep level. You may not be aware of what you are currently resonating at a deep level, but it is vitally important that you do so that you can 'retune your frequency' if necessary. This is why self-awareness is so important and we will focus on that in the next section of the book.

The Meaning of Life

'In the long run we are all dead.'
J.M. Keynes

What's life about? Strip out everything from our lives and what's the point? We all end up dead anyway, so why bother? When we step back and consider this, we realise that the only reason we would bother with the struggle of life is if on some deep level we were aware that the game we are playing is actually bigger than us. We play a part, but that's not it – there's more to it than just our lifespan. The game continues after we are gone.

The meaning of life is widely touted as the ultimate profound question that no one can answer. When you take the perspective of the One paradigm it becomes remarkably clear and simple. Nature is the greatest power, so we look there for the answer. I think this quote from Richard Mabey sums it up nicely:

'It's quite plain that, on our planet at least, the evolved solution to life was to invent as many organisms as possible to exploit the great variety of climates and geological niches, and to buffer us against change.'
Richard Mabey, *Planet Earth: The Future*[10]

Simply put, the meaning of life is to perpetuate life and enable evolution to create more variety. That is what it has been doing over millions of years. However, the modern world we have created is actually destroying the variety of species and habitats. No wonder we are feeling psychologically stressed; the way we are living is directly contradicting the very meaning of life.

If you care for and nurture all life, it evolves over time to create more variety. The longer this goes on, the more evolved and intricate the relationships become between a greater variety of species, and the more balance is preserved through multiple species and relationships.

Life on our planet began in the seas and the largest mammals are found there – along with the most evolved and potent poisons. You only have to dive on one of the great coral reefs of the world to witness an incredible array of interdependency in the spectacular multicoloured communities of fish, molluscs and other creatures that support each other.

The meaning of life implies that we should naturally want to care for our own life, the life of our species and the natural lives of other species around us because they all support us. The aborigines of Northern Australia led a tough existence in a harsh environment, but they demonstrated expertise in this area. Studies have shown that where aborigines lived, the natural biodiversity around them actually *increased*. The way they lived in and managed the natural environment around them was so ingrained in natural power it increased variety, increased quantity and buffered them against change. If they could do it, I'm sure we can if we put our minds to it.

Working through Maslow's hierarchy of needs in your life, once you reach the self-actualisation level, you begin to become aware that your life purpose is part of a bigger game. Leaving the world a better place than when you came into it becomes more important to you. You hope that your legacy is positive, your children will achieve more than you did in your lifetime and the world's average will have been raised just slightly by what you did while you were here. Can you imagine any sane person saying, 'I want to leave the world worse than I found it and I hope my offspring don't do as well as me'?

When it comes to our own species, the opportunities for enabling the 'evolution' part of the meaning of life are immense. With such a complex and intelligent being, we have numerous interrelated structures of communities, cultures, commerce, art, science, technology, education, language, leisure, behaviour and just about everything else you can think of. At the pinnacle of human development, self-actualisation, paying attention to helping the evolution of our species becomes more compelling. Deep fulfilment lies here.

- *How do you care for life and enable evolution?*
- *What aspects of the way you live actually damage life and limit evolution (physically, culturally or in some other way)?*
- *What aspect of our human evolution are you personally here to contribute to?*

It is natural for you to continually evolve and develop on your journey towards your highest potential. We will work more on the answers to these, some of life's ultimate questions, in the next section of this book.

Natural Patterns

Patterns demonstrate many other ways in which natural power moves. Take for example the continually subdividing shape of a tree. This pattern is repeated in the shape of river deltas viewed from the air and vein networks in your body. It appears in the connections of social relationships such as organisational structures as well as the links between your friends and acquaintances. It is a natural pattern.

Another example is a spiral. It occurs on a snail shell, in a tornado and in the water going down a plug hole. The same pattern turns up psychologically in terms of vicious cycles of abuse and the spiralling debt of someone going bankrupt, and you will notice the same pattern when we talk about how beliefs create self-fulfilling prophecies in the next section of the book.

When working with wood, if you plane with the grain, you glean smooth strips and easily produce a fine finish. If you work against the grain, it is not natural. The plane bumps and grates across the wood. The finish is poor and requires much more work to get it looking anywhere near as good. Understanding natural patterns enables you to work with the grain of nature, effortlessly achieving more of a higher quality in your life.

- *The next time you notice a natural pattern, consider how it could have relevance to a situation in your life.*
- *What is the natural lesson that either explains why something is happening or acts as a potential solution to an issue?*
- *Decide on a positive action that would be acting 'with the grain' of the natural pattern. Notice what happens as a result.*

Look for patterns. Notice how they turn up physically, in your psyche and between people. If you notice and utilise them, then you are behaving in the same way that power moves naturally in the world. If you work with natural patterns, you work with nature. You work with the grain of the most powerful force in the world. You effortlessly begin to unleash more of the latent natural power that resides within you.

Human Nature: What's Important?

The second important aspect of nature is what is natural for us as a species. Consider the 24-hour clock that we created earlier.

- *What did your human ancestors (recent as they are) spend most of their time doing?*
- *For thousands of years, what actions do you think made them feel happy and fulfilled?*
- *Compare that with how you spend your time. How different is it?*
- *How many of your waking hours do you spend on comparatively recent, artificial things that demand*

attention in the modern world (for example driving, computers, TV etc.)?

We have already mentioned log fires. Why do you think we find something comforting in them? I think it is because for hundreds of thousands of years our species sat round them in family groups communicating with each other, feeling safe from the dangerous world outside and strengthening bonds. In comparison, the television has been around for 70 years – that's less than 0.01% of the time.

- *How much time do you spend each week sitting round a fire, talking with your close family and friends? When you do it (perhaps once a year at Christmas) what is it like?*
- *How much time do you spend watching TV? What do you get from it? How does the TV you watch make you feel compared to the comforting nature of your family sitting around a fire?*
- *What messages do you most often get from the TV programmes you watch? Are they positive ones that make you feel good? If not, what are the messages you tend to receive?*
- *How do these messages perpetuate the modern world view of separateness rather than the One perspective that everything is related and interconnected?*

I found something deeply satisfying about canoeing along the Zambezi when I was looking out over enormous flocks of wild birds and an obviously thriving ecosystem. I thought to myself, 'Is it really too much to suspect that along with the comforting fire, somewhere deep in my DNA is a part of my ancestors for whom this would have represented pure bliss; an abundant water supply, agreeable climate and a bountiful food source?'

Reconnecting with nature in this way made me feel really good at a deep level. But for there to be something in this idea there would need to be some way of your body 'remembering' things from generations before.

The Memory of Cells

When I discussed this with my brother who is a geneticist, he drew my attention to a paper he had recently read in *The Scientist*.[11]

As the Second World War drew to a close the Germans imposed a food embargo on an area of Western Holland that caused 30,000 people to die of starvation. Scientists recently studied the descendants of the people who survived this episode. When they compared them to a 'control' population (i.e. one that had not been subjected to starvation in the past), they discovered subtle differences in the protein deposits they found in their cells.

Following rigorous scientific study, the conclusion was startling. The scientists found that something remains in our cells following an experience in our life. Not just a mental memory, but a physical one too. Not only this, but it is passed down to successive generations. Children who were born long after these hard years still had a physical 'memory' of the starvation episode experienced by their parents and grandparents.

The rational conclusion is that similar 'memories' have been deposited within you over thousands and thousands of years. It seems that there are subtle physical 'memories' within you of all your ancestors (human and pre-human). This physical lineage connecting us back to our forefathers helps to define what is known as 'human nature'. No one else has exactly the same 'nature' as you individually, but in the big scheme of things everyone shares a vastly similar background as a species. Again, the similarities of human nature far outweigh the differences.

Logically, there is something deep within you that, no matter how small, connects back up your family tree to that ultimate first spark of life that occurred in the world. Some call this 'source'. We all share this profound and inescapable speck of source. This 'memory' defines what life is. If you can listen to human nature and understand it, you get to understand what it means to be human.

The Ultimate Danger

'300 years ago only 10% of the world's population lived in cities. A century ago it was a quarter. Today it's a half. By the middle of the century it will be two thirds and that makes for changes and stresses and pressures.'
Robert May, *Planet Earth: The Future*[12]

I went to Singapore Zoo once and saw a polar bear. He looked happy and energetic. I watched him walk along, swinging his head. He knocked a tyre with his nose and jumped into the water, swimming backstroke, just brushing his nose under an overhang, flipping over and paddling to the side where he got out and shook himself dry. Often when I go to a zoo I see animals just sitting around looking depressed, so this was a real joy.

There was a large group of enthralled people watching the bear's antics. People came and went as I stood there for some time marvelling at the world's biggest land-based carnivore. Then I became aware that something was wrong. Somehow this was too perfect. Then I realised what it was. My enthrallment became sadness as the bear repeated exactly the same routine time after time after time. Prolonged imprisonment in his enclosure had affected his mental health and had driven him to display repeated obsessive behaviours.

I've thought of that bear often since and the analogy between him and many people's current modern-day lives is frighteningly close. Let's take the example of a businessman who is unhappy in his job. He is woken by an artificial alarm clock, turns on artificial lighting, goes for an artificial shower, eats an artificial breakfast, goes to work on artificial transport, sits in an artificial building all day looking at an artificial computer screen doing an artificial job that is artificial to him because it is against his nature, before artificially travelling back to his artificially built house to watch artificial TV and going to sleep in an artificial bed.

I have lived this life. I didn't even notice that it was sunny on the hottest day of the year because my office and car were air conditioned. I had become almost completely removed from what was natural for a human being. Rather than being close to human nature, I was living in an artificial enclosure. I felt trapped doing something that was not natural to me. On a deep level I may as well have been in a prison. I didn't know it then, but I was on my way to becoming that polar bear.

Living against the grain of human nature is stressful. In my artificial life I didn't like my job, but enjoyed my weekends, so I lost 5:2 every week. That was a drumming. Some people I know have to play golf on Saturday morning to unwind otherwise they snap at the children and their wife due to the stresses they endure in the week. Sunday night blues also kick in before the end of the weekend. The misery of working against the grain of human nature then encroaches significantly on the weekend, making the score more like 6:1.

How many 6:1 losses in a row does it take to push someone over the edge? How long before they become the polar bear, going through the motions in a dazed dream-like state to deaden the discomfort of being trapped in an artificial enclosure? How long before nature deals a blow to forcibly restore the balance? If this sounds like you or someone you know, it is time to wake up before it is too late. Rather than focusing on maintaining the standard of your prison, it is time to break out of it.

Personal Nature: Happiness is a Natural Guide

'Success is not the key to happiness. Happiness is the key to success.
If you love what you are doing, you will be successful.'
Herman Cain

Why does happiness feel good?

I think it is because it is nature's way. Happiness feels good because it must be good for us … really good! It is well known that when you laugh and are happy, your body releases positive chemicals and endorphins that help to keep you well. If something makes you feel happy, it is natural to do it. That's how your brain works, it's natural. As Susan Scott says in *Fierce Conversations*, 'our radar works perfectly. It is the operator who is in question.'[13]

Ask yourself why you do something. Like a child, with each answer you come up with, keep on asking, 'Why?' Eventually this process bottoms out somewhere. If it bottoms out at 'because it makes me really happy', then that would seem to be natural and good for you. If it bottoms out anywhere else, question it. 'Because I feel I should' is not good enough. 'Because it's expected of me' is not good enough. 'Because I need to' is not good enough. Only 'Because it makes me happy' will do.

The Desiderata has a lovely line at the end of it. It simply says: 'Strive to be happy.'

You have a short time in this world. It is natural to seek out what makes you happy and spend your time there. What makes you happy is different from what makes other people happy and that is fine. It is natural. Imagine if everyone wanted to do the same job, marry the same person, have the same lifestyle and live in the same place – what a nightmare! It is natural for us to seek out what comes naturally to our own personal nature. This fits within the context of the larger scale perspective of human nature and the holistic view of all nature.

It could be that being an accountant suits your personal nature. It could that being a sports coach suits you, or being a cleaner. You could be here to work part time, full time or no time. You could be here to raise children. There are a myriad of lives and jobs that are vital to the successful operation of our community and the evolution of our species, whether directly or in a supporting role. All are vital. The key is finding out which of these is most in line with your personal nature. What comes naturally to you?

As you start to appreciate the natural world, human nature and your own personal nature, you begin to get a sense of not only the macro-scale journey that mankind is on, but also the personal journey that you have been on within it, right up to the point where you are reading these exact words right now.

With this in mind your natural future can start to become clearer. Meaning can emerge into your life. You are able to approach each day focusing on what is natural to you, rather than 'forcing' something that may not represent your natural journey.

Now that you have the foundations of One, you are well poised to embark on a profound journey towards self-actualisation. If you have got this far, you understand why we are where we are and you understand the key themes of the One paradigm:

- *Everything is related*
- *Everything is connected*
- *Nature is the greatest power*

Now that you understand the three basic foundations of One, the second half of this book guides you through an approach that will enable you to bring the One perspective to life so that you can live in it every day. You will build your awareness so that you can:

- *Understand your history, what you are resonating in the zero point field and why*
- *Accept the past and turn your focus to the present moment, including retuning your frequency if appropriate*
- *Tune your resonance to the ultimate level, bringing more of what you deeply desire into your life*
- *Listen to the zero point field and learn how to read the messages there for you*
- *Live a happier and more fulfilling life*
- *Begin to understand your life purpose, the meaning of your life in context of the whole*
- *Transform your leadership of the One paradigm*
- *Prepare yourself for the power you are likely to unleash as you start living up to your true potential*

Part 2

Unleash The Power

The Map

In this part of the book, the One paradigm is used to assist you on the ultimate journey towards self-actualisation – a journey that will unleash the power of your true potential. It would be trite and shallow to assume that you could publish a simple guide for everyone to follow and if a map for this journey was truly that simple it would have been published long ago. In this respect each of us is venturing into uncharted territory. It seems as if every corner of our world has been discovered and mapped. Often it seems as if there is no adventure left any more. How apt then that one of the most incredibly challenging journeys left to humankind is the personal journey of self-awareness and self-actualisation.

The journey to unleash the power of your true potential is as unique as you are. The paths that you decide to take or not take will be different to everyone else's. You have also come to this exact moment by unique means. No one else will have taken the same journey as you through life so far.

Despite the fact that everyone's journey is unique, there are clues that help to signpost the way. In the leadership work I do with clients there seem to be broad similarities, which you would expect as we are all part of One inter-related, interconnected living system. In this part of the book I will share pointers and exercises that will enable you to begin to create your own map and take steps along it. I will bring the ideas to life with personal experiences – either my own or those of the people I have been privileged to meet on parts of this journey.

We are going to delve into human nature ... your human nature.

Before we do, a warning: this can be a difficult journey. You need to be ready for it. You need to be ready to face your darkest fears and secrets. I recommend that you go through the challenges with a professional coach for support and guidance along the way. Please do not attempt this journey if you are not creative, resourceful and whole.

To prepare for the journey, first we need to appreciate the importance of 'resonance' and then we need to define where we are going with this 'true potential' of ours.

The Power of Resonance

There is much that still needs to be discovered about quantum physics including details of the energy that connects everything, but it has something to do with wave-lengths. Wavelengths are the shape of the 'wave' that emanates from all particles, just like the radio waves that are picked up in your home when you listen to your favourite radio station. When two waves match each other, they are said to 'resonate' (they are 'in tune'); if two waves clash, they 'dissonate'. You can hear this in sound waves when something is either in or out of tune to your ear. It is the same kind of thing with the energy that connects everything through the zero point field.

There is however more power to wavelengths than just sound. Everything has a wavelength. Even stationary inanimate objects have a wavelength about them, which would be no surprise given the findings of quantum physics. Have you ever seen TV footage of a 'solid' suspension bridge rolling wildly in a gale? This phenomenon happens when the wavelength of the wind just happens to exactly match the wavelength of the bridge itself. If wavelengths match, they join together, deepening the troughs and building the peaks. They become more and more pronounced until they start to physically affect things; in this instance moving a solid bridge. Continue this for long enough and you can get spectacular results.

My granddad has played the organ at his local parish

church for 50 years. When he presses the 'lower C' pedal, the regulars on the front pew lean forward and hold the organ's casing. This is because the wavelength of the organ's wooden casing resonates at lower C and it starts to rattle. They lean forward and push on it to stop it rattling. The same phenomenon occurs when an opera singer hits a high note and is able to shatter glass.

Resonance is extremely important. It is a physical, scientifically proven phenomenon – it is not magic. It has the power to move bridges and to change your life if you choose to embrace its power. It is very, very real.

As we look at the ultimate journey of the individual to his or her highest potential within the context of the One paradigm, we will talk about resonance a lot. The particles that you are physically made up of are sending out signals right now, even though you may not be aware of them. They have a 'wavelength'. They will be either resonating or dissonating with your actions. If you tend to act 'against the grain', you dissonate and disperse your energy. If you act naturally with it you increase its strength, unleashing great power; the power of your true potential.

Do not underestimate the power of what you are resonating right now. What you are currently resonating attracted this book into your hands. I said at the start that you co-created the moment when you looked at the first page of this book. This is why. You would not be reading these words now if you were not resonating that the time is right.

Resonance can be incredibly useful. Remember the law of attraction? You will tend to get what you resonate (good or bad), so shedding light on what you resonate and 'tuning' your resonance as appropriate will be more likely to bring you what you truly, deeply need. Not only will you be consciously choosing which of life's dice you want to throw next, but you start to be able to weight them in your favour too.

Your resonance through the naturally occurring zero point field not only attracted this book into your hands, but you and thousands of other people like you actually helped to create the book itself in the first place. I'll explain how later. Now that you understand the power of resonance, it's time to identify where you are heading; your true potential.

Your True Potential: Where is it?

The *Collins Dictionary* definition of potential is 'possible, but not yet actual ... capable of being, but latent'. If something is 'latent' it is present, but dormant; it is not obvious or explicit. It is not yet revealed or manifest. So what is it that is within you and points to your true potential right now, without being explicit?

As Maslow suggested, there are various versions of us that are invoked depending on circumstances. For example, a professional businessperson deprived of food and shelter for a few days would become a different version of themselves. There is nothing wrong with this. It is a 'lower' version of you on the pyramid, but it is natural.

The current level you are likely to be at is the ego level, so this is the version of 'you' that you are most likely to identify with. You can hear your ego as the voice within your head. It chats away most of the time. It draws on memories of the past and makes plans for the future. It defines roles. It makes sense of situations. Its purpose is to build self-esteem. It feeds off other people. How it is perceived by others is important to its health.

You may well believe that your ego IS you. If this is the case, your ego will feel safe. It will read these words and say, 'Hang on! What's he talking about here? Is this implying that there is more than one version of me? That's clearly not the case. I don't understand. I am the voice that is reading these words. That is me, not some so-called "ego thing".'

There is however a 'higher level' of us; the apex of Maslow's hierarchy and of human development. This book will guide you as you cast light on it, begin to understand it and invoke it. It has been called many things. It is difficult to define and many words used have been misused and therefore carry negative baggage with them. Even by naming it, in a way you attempt to define it and categorise it, therefore putting an unhelpful ego onto it.

Of course the word itself does not matter, but we need to refer to something so that we can unleash its potential. Maslow calls the apex of his hierarchy 'self-actualisation'; the achievement of purpose. It is known in some circles as your 'higher self', in others as your 'heart', 'spirit' or 'soul'. Use whatever term you prefer. I will interchange them for they all point to the same thing. If a term I use has negative baggage for you, just replace it with the word that resonates most naturally for you.

Please now leave any baggage at the door as we walk out onto the hallowed turf of the human soul.

You Got Soul

The term 'soul' has been around for centuries. The *Collins Dictionary* definition is 'the spirit or immaterial part of man, the seat of human personality, intellect, will and emotions; the essential part or fundamental nature of anything'. No surprise that we bump into that vital term 'nature' here again.

When we were born we had no ego; we did not think. I have seen people's faces light up just at the sight of a baby. There is no ego about babies, just the innocent soul, shining forth for all to see. This can be incredibly engaging.

As we grow the innocent soul is subjected to experiences: some happy, some sad, some mundane, some incredibly painful. As a natural process, the ego starts to build around the soul to protect it through these difficult times. It takes its experiences of the world and attributes labels to them. It categorises things. It creates systems and processes to enable it to make sense of the world and to get through difficult times.

Over time it can smother the soul. It is as if we start out as a beautiful, sparkling, brilliant-cut diamond and then spend many years plastering over it to protect it. As we stick rocks and lumps of earth over it to shelter it, we only catch glimpses of the beauty and power that lie beneath. As we reach our teenage years, most of us are highly egocentric and take that approach into our first jobs. Most traditional views on human development end there. You are eighteen; you are now an adult, that's it! Next stop: death.

A hundred years ago when times were harder, there may have been little chance to develop to your highest potential, because environmental factors kept you lower down the pyramid. Life was harder then. The world was at a lower stage of Maslow's hierarchy of needs.

Now, however, the Western world has enjoyed years of stability. There is a solid platform for us to achieve self-actualisation of our soul; our deeper presence, if we are brave enough to take on the journey. This journey means gently peeling back the layers of ego and chipping off those layers of earth to uncover our deeper self, our brilliant-cut diamond. Once we are more aware of the diamond within us, we can choose to act in alignment with it. This brings the extraordinary power of the resonance of the soul to bear on your life.

That means bringing your vulnerable heart out to play again.

Some clients I work with are so removed from their heart or soul that they cannot remember what they love to do anymore. Some are at a point where their soul is so longing to be let out from the tight cage they have trapped it in for so long, that a few questions about values and life direction cause a deep emotional reaction. On the outside they appear as successful businesspeople because the ego is well catered for.

Last week it was as if the pressure on one client's soul was so great that it literally squeezed out through the tears in her eyes. She was a successful businesswoman, but she was living a life that was cut off from her soul. She was therefore living a soulless life, which fed her ego well. The ego was happy, the soul was not. She was therefore struggling with a deep sense of dis-ease.

The Ego Trap

Most people act in line with what the ego demands. Often what your ego wants to get out of life is not in line with what your soul wants to get out of life. When we are out of whack with our soul we dissonate in the zero point field; our energy is dispersed and our impact reduced. No hope of us moving bridges from here.

There are some clues that suggest someone may be out of alignment. They can come across as overly positive or overly negative about things – either way they somehow seem unable to see the truth. Their words and actions may be at odds. Their rhetoric may not add up. They may come across as hypocritical or defensive. They may play out a role, identifying with that rather than their true soul – what it means to them to be human. They may get stuck in the same patterns of behaviour that produce a predictable cause and effect. They may attract the wrong kind of people into their lives over and over again. Try as they might on the surface of things, they somehow just don't seem to make much progress on a deep level.

The closer you are to alignment, the more these kind of behaviours stand out and dissonate. You notice them in yourself and others – you develop greater awareness. The more out of alignment you are yourself, the more the ego blinds you to this kind of behaviour in yourself and others. You just don't see it.

As you can imagine, living this kind of life is incredibly stressful. The ego is paddling furiously beneath the water to keep up the pretence that all is well to the outside world. The problem is that the modern world paradigm values the ego over the soul. Success is often based on egoic measures as today's 'celebrity culture' demonstrates.

With the increasingly secular approach of the West, we have been left in a spiritual vacuum. No one is asking us what our soul wants out of life any more. We are better placed than we have ever been before in history to take a step up. Maslow's more basic needs are well catered for. We ought to be ascending, but without someone asking us life's big questions, we are left where we are. Without a viable map that we can buy into, we don't know the way. With a society that seems to value money and the ego, we think we've 'made it'. We continue to seek motivation in an area where our needs have long been fully met. We become imprisoned in the ego trap.

We get caught between a rock and a hard place. On the one hand we want more out of life, but on the other there seems so much to lose. Getting more in touch with and revealing our vulnerable soul is daunting. The ego ensures that we are fearful and tells us, 'Better the devil you know. Things aren't that bad.'

When the ego outstays its welcome an imbalance is created within us. We get a nagging suspicion that there must be more to life than this. Unknowingly we begin to take out an overdraft on ourselves. We tend to sit and wait, making the most out of the ego-dominated world we live in while we do. Meanwhile the pressure builds.

Nature is the greatest power. One of nature's rules is about the importance of balance. Key warning signs that things are out of balance are depression and stress. That is why the WHO's prediction is so ominous. The WHO says that things are going to get worse before they get better. My fear is that if people who are ready to ascend into the self-actualisation level don't make a conscious choice to go on this journey in time, nature will force them to. Nature forced me to. If I can save one person having to be forced through that journey and the dangers it presents, then the years spent bringing this book into existence will have been worthwhile.

So that's the bad news, forcing us to set sail on this trepidous journey. What's the good news tempting us to our destination?

The Graceful Digger

When someone is living in alignment with their inner higher self, their soul and ego are aligned. Their actions are consistent with their words. They are at level 3 awareness of many things and as a result they have a certain authenticity about what they do. The wavelengths in all aspects of their life are aligned and resonate strongly. They often have presence, gravitas and a positive energy about them. When they do what they are here to do it is often like watching poetry in motion. They make difficult tasks look simple. They achieve fantastic results with relative ease. They are happy and fulfilled, as are those who come into contact with them in this mode. It is infectious.

Two people could say exactly the same thing, one from the heart and one just going through the motions. If one's ego and soul are not aligned to the words, it falls flat. It is inauthentic. Everyone has an innate human ability to sniff out the dissonance of inauthentic people at work and we don't trust them.

The one who speaks with authenticity is the one who is more likely to move people to action. Authenticity is a fascinating thing. Although it would be difficult to describe how to spot authenticity, we all have an inbuilt radar that can pick up on the resonating wavelengths caused by it.

Great things are achieved when you act in alignment with your soul. You unleash the power of your true potential. It spills out everywhere. You resonate true deep power, not surface ego ripples. You have the power to rock bridges.

When a gifted sports person does what it is that they love, you catch glimpses of this. Some gifted orators have the ability to emotionally move huge numbers of people. Some politicians have changed the world. The thing is it does not *have* to be at this level. Everyone can't be a world-changing politician (thank goodness!). You can find people acting in this way in all walks of life.

On a family shopping trip, my son wanted to watch the workmen who were digging up the street. My wife went off to make progress on the shopping list whilst I stood next to my son, peering through the metal gates that protected pedestrians. At first it seemed just a normal building site, but then through the hustle and bustle of this unlikely scene, something beautiful emerged.

There was a central role in that building site – that of the man in the digger. The mechanical arm was digging holes with great skill, scraping exactly the right amount of earth up to leave an almost perfectly level surface. The scoop gracefully opened, spreading the earth out evenly on the mound. Every now and then when something needed to be lifted from one location to another, the arm magically appeared right next to the individual, who then attached it. The heavy weight then swung through the air and landed softly in exactly the right place.

When a man driving a roller could not get up a ramp, the bucket arrived immediately and gently pushed him up the hill, causing the driver to smile. There was an incredible efficiency about the site. People around the digger seemed happy and were whistling cheerfully as they went about their work.

I looked at the operator and saw a happy and contented look on his face. He was completely absorbed in his work, but this seemed to be work with a capital 'W'. There seemed to be nothing 'hard' about this work for him. He clearly loved what he was doing and received a large amount of fulfilment from the task itself. It seemed as if his body and soul were in alignment. He was doing what he was here to do. He was truly in the moment.

I caught his eye. 'You are very graceful with that digger!' I shouted to him above the noise of the machinery. It seemed rather a strange thing to say to a workman, but he smiled at me and mouthed 'Thank you' with a knowing look in his eye.

So you see you don't have to be the prime minister to unleash the power of your true potential – that would be the ego talking. What you need to do is develop more under-standing. You need to know:

1 *What your unconscious soul is resonating.*
2 *What your ego is resonating.*
3 *How to bring them together in harmony so that they resonate with full power.*

If you feel happy, content and fulfilled on a deep level about where you are on your life's journey right now, then these three points are probably in pretty close alignment whether you are a workman driving a digger or the prime minister. If that is not the case (and you can be honest with yourself here because you are reading a book on your own and no one else will know what you think), then something may have to give if you really want to unleash the power of your true potential.

Unless you are living in line with the journey towards your true potential right now, your soul will be (to a greater or lesser extent) ruled by your ego. To enable your soul to emerge from the background to play a more central role in your life and to unleash its great power, the ego needs to learn to step aside. If you are heavily identified with your ego, it may feel as if you yourself will need to step aside.

Welcome to your Two-million-bit Processor

Scientists have concluded that your conscious mind can deal with about seven bits of information at once. We trust our conscious mind because it tends to talk in the language of the modern world. It tends to be tangible, based on rational arguments, and uses a language we easily understand. It is highly useful and we could not live without it. It is also where the ego resides.

Your unconscious mind however can deal with two million bits of information at once. This is where the soul resides. It has the most incredible power, but it doesn't tend to talk in the language of the modern world paradigm. Your unconscious soul tends to communicate through things like pictures, feelings, emotions and intuitions. The ego is like the seven-bit operator of a two-million-bit computer that is sending out messages in a foreign language on the screen.

You can often receive a very clear message from your unconscious, but it may need some translating to make sense of it. This translation puts the ego off – 'What if I get the translation wrong?' – and it therefore often ignores the message. In many cases the ego has actually turned off the soul processor or ignores it completely.

There is something profound about your unconscious. We all have an unconscious mind, but as individuals we rarely understand it. How can we act in alignment with it if we don't understand it? The more we understand it, the more accurately the ego can translate the messages it has for us. The more we use it, the better we get at it. It is time to start learning its language and listening to it.

Think about it. How much more successful could someone be if they could effectively use their two-million-bit processor versus someone who could only use their seven-bit processor? I make it about two hundred thousand times more successful.

Now there's a reason to embark on a difficult journey.

To unleash the power of your true potential, you have to understand messages from your subconscious soul. You have to understand what it is resonating. You can then choose to act in accordance with that.

Say Hello Again to Your Soul

I think it is important to 'experience' and not just 'understand'. You may know exactly what I am talking about here, or you may not. If not, here is an exercise that may help you to get an idea about the part of you that is your soul.

Sit down in a quiet place. Take some deep breaths. Relax. Listen to the voice inside your head. Listen to your ego. It is not inherently good or inherently bad, it just is. Don't worry when thoughts pop into your head, just notice them. Notice the feeling of them popping into your head. Notice where they come from.

The voice is not totally you, is it?

There is more to you than just this voice. If there wasn't, you would not be able to notice it as *it* would be all you are. There would be no other perspective to observe it from.

If you are finding this a bit hard to get your head around, I completely understand. It is a difficult thing to explain. Twenty-five years ago, I remember someone holding up a square piece of paper with a black dot on it in a school assembly.

'What do you see?' they asked.
'A black dot,' we all replied.
'Good. Anything else?'
We looked hard. We tried to interpret the dot in different ways. We considered all sorts of possible creative answers to this trick question. We were going nowhere.
'Does no one see a white square?'

The ego-voice is the dot. The soul is the white canvas on which the ego paints its picture. It is the screen that the ego sends its emails across. It is the silence over which the ego voice is heard. It is on the one hand hugely significant, profound and vital. Without it you would have no means upon which the ego could be founded. Without it you have nothing. Yet when it is there, its quiet presence is easily missed.

I was unaware of this element of myself and had a very egoic 'busy mind'. I found it hard to 'shut down'. I had tried meditating, but I just sat there thinking of more things to do.

I was being coached by a colleague around this issue and we were trying to work out different approaches. I tend to like pictures and find it easy to shut my eyes and envision things, but of course there was nothing I could picture here. That was the point; I was trying to clear my mind of everything. I thought that the best I could do was envisage being in a pure white room.

I closed my eyes and pictured it. My ego stuck a pure white sofa in it to sit on, so I had to get rid of that along with the white lilies in a white vase. The walls had to go too. As I got rid of more and more things, eventually I was able to just picture myself surrounded by pure white. My breathing slowed. I relaxed. Possibly for the first time ever in my life I achieved a quiet state of mind; a stillness I had not encountered before.

Then in my mind's eye a pale shadow in the shape of a small head popped up in front of me. It came from somewhere else in my subconscious – I did not seem to be in control of it. It seemed to be looking at me inquisitively, as if it was not used to visitors. It had a child-like feeling about it. I felt very emotional.

It felt as if I had just come face to face with my soul for the first time in my life.

Poor thing.

It had been hanging out in the white room all alone for thirty-five years.

The Journey

There are two things to consider on the first part of this journey. What your deeper soul is resonating and what your ego is resonating. It is hard even to define the human soul, let alone explicitly map out what it is resonating, but we will undertake exercises that will point to it. The thresholds between what is conscious and unconscious or ego and soul are also blurred. There is no easy definition that clearly distinguishes between them.

This is a true adventure. You are about to set out with a sketchy idea of what you are looking for and we will be filling in the map as we go.

In spiritual texts it often seems to be implied that you can 'achieve' a state of nirvana or fulfilment. Buddhism talks of 'achieving enlightenment' and there is a danger that in today's world we translate that as an end point where we can put our feet up. You cannot achieve fulfilment; however you can lead a fulfilling life. You cannot achieve enlightenment; but you can lead an enlightened and enlightening life. You do not reach an end point, punch the air and shout, 'Yes I did it!' You enjoy the walk down the road towards fulfilling your life purpose.

I have heard of people achieving a godlike state of consciousness where they truly appreciate the oneness of all things. I think there is a danger that we think all spiritual enlightenment happens with a huge kaboom! I also think there is a danger that we consider spiritual enlightenment to be the preserve of holy men who dedicate their entire lives to the cause.

There is a lot you can do to bring more of your soul into your life. You can live a happier more fulfilling life without dedicating hours of it to meditation. You can draw on its enormous inherent power in your life without having to go to church every Sunday. That doesn't mean it is easy, we are just accessing it through a different channel – that of the One paradigm of quantum physics.

Some people fall into what they are here to do without any consideration of the questions we will be asking in the next chapter. Lucky them! Millions of people don't. It is a simple matter of rolling life's dice again. Some people get lucky, most don't. We are about to choose some dice with better odds for you. Of course there is no guarantee that you will unleash the power of your true potential. I know that upon finishing this book, some of you will. Many of you will make some hugely beneficial changes and a few of you will not. That's life dice. Which one do you think you will be?

The next chapter will enable you to build your self-awareness so you can start to understand which dice your soul wants to roll. Then you are able to assess to what extent you are living in alignment with that. We will peel back some of the onion skin layers of your ego to shed some light on what you are resonating.

- *Are you acting with the grain and building your power or are you ignoring it and ploughing a more difficult furrow?*
- *Is life easy for you or hard work?*
- *Do perfect opportunities just seem to drop in your lap or do you always seem to miss the boat?*
- *Are people moved by what you say or do your words seem to slip off them like water from a duck's back?*

It is time to shed light on these questions and more.

You Are a Transmitter

Quantum physicists discovered that subatomic particles existed in a state of perpetual potential. They also discovered that they only assumed a defined state when they were observed. There was something about being observed and measured that actually made them cease their 'potential' state and adopt an 'actual' one.

In the 1960s as a research physicist at Boeing Scientific Research Laboratories, Helmut Schmidt conducted experiments to ascertain the extent of this.[14] In one example of his work two individuals seemed to be able to influence a Random Number Generator that produced either a 'heads' or 'tails' result, like flipping a coin. A lady and a man were asked to focus on influencing the machine to produce more heads than tails. In repeated tests the lady scored more heads than was statistically normal. Surprisingly the man came up with more tails than was statistically normal.

In repeated tests, the lady scored heads 52.5% of the time. The man scored heads 47.75% of the time. This may not seem like much of a difference to you, but the statistical probability of this occurring by chance was more than ten million to one. There's another one of those coincidences that should make you sit up and pay attention. Why did the man score the opposite of what he was supposed to be focusing on? Could it be that although his surface ego was wishing for 'heads', it was not aligned with his deeper more powerful two-million-bit processor of the unconscious?

There's a 5% difference between these two results. If you relate this to life, then for every twenty positive events one person co-created, another could co-create 21. That is a significant advantage in the modern world. Imagine loading your dice 5% in your favour on every roll.

This was a shock for the scientific community. Far from scientists being independent, it would seem that they actually had an influence on what happened even in scientifically controlled experiments. It was as if they were 'vibrating' an energy that encouraged particles at this most basic of levels to take on a certain form.

If we apply this to you and your life then we come up with a startling prospect: depending on what you deeply resonate, you can increase your chances of attracting more of what you want into your life.

- *Do you know what signals you are sending out right now?*

It is incredibly important that you do. On one level you are able to co-create what turns up in your life. You are attracting things into your life that depend on what you are resonating. Do you know someone who always seems to attract 'users' in their relationships? Could it be that on one level they are unwittingly inviting these kind of people into their life?

Just like the local parish organ, the wavelengths you are sending out will resonate or dissonate with other people and objects. Whilst you may *consciously* choose which of life's dice you want to roll, you may *unconsciously* be loading your dice through what you are *unconsciously* resonating at a deeper level. You have the capacity to load your dice, to increase the probability of attracting certain events into your life and repelling others. Of course you cannot fully control anything – that would not be natural and nature is the greatest power, but you can certainly choose which of life's dice you want to roll *and* then load them.

No one can sprinkle fairy dust on you and do this for you. Other people will certainly help you on your journey, but it is down to you. Only you can choose this path. Only you can start to load life's dice by increasing your self-awareness; by becoming conscious; by becoming fully present to yourself.

If you are consciously and unconsciously resonating something clearly and acting with the grain at level 3 awareness, then it is easy for events, people and things that are in tune with that wavelength to effortlessly come into your life. It is just natural for them to do so and nature is the greatest power.

It is important to know what is working for you (remember you are an evolutionary winner, so lots of things will be going right!) so that you can make the most out of these areas. It is also important to know how you may be getting in the way of your own success so that you can 'retune' your vibration as necessary.

- *What do you think is holding you back from achieving your true potential?*

To uncover this, you need to deepen your self-awareness.

We need to shed some light on the stranger self of your soul.

You Are an Iceberg

I have news for you; you are an iceberg.

If you and I were to look at each other, we would only see the things that are apparent on the surface. This is broadly limited to appearance and behaviour (what we say and what we do). Behaviour is easy to observe, as are its effects, but what drives behaviour is more difficult to understand and can't be seen.

What do we know about icebergs? Most of their bulk lies unseen beneath the surface and they are a danger to shipping. So it is true of what drives our behaviour. Beneath the surface lie the conscious and unconscious psychological drivers of our behaviour. These are deep things that only you can know and yet very few people are actually consciously aware of them within themselves. They are things like genetics, upbringing, past experience, friends, family, hopes, fears, expectations, beliefs, emotions, religion, values, personality and motivators.

At its deepest level, right at the base of the iceberg is your life purpose – what you are here to do. Most people never find out what this is. Few even look. This is where we are going. Be aware that the journey to uncovering your life purpose is often a life-long exercise and not one that can be easily deciphered simply by reading a book. It will require significant personal work by you if you are to find the way. Work that only you can put in; work that you will only put in if you are truly ready for the journey.

Remember also that the journey is the point.

Being 'on the right road' is the destination.

You could be there right now if you decided to.

I stood on the deck of a Russian research vessel called the *Academic Ioffe* in a stretch of the Antarctic Ocean known as Iceberg Alley. Antarctica is the windiest continent on earth and a hundred-mile-an-hour katabatic wind was tearing at my back. The hood of my coat flapped wildly about my face as I clung onto the hand rail. Despite this the iceberg that I was watching moved eerily against the wind towards me. This was because with so much of its bulk lying beneath the surface of the water, it did not matter which way the wind blew. Icebergs always move with the current. So it is with us.

Much personal development work is tactical and focuses on behaviour. It chips away at what we can see on the surface of the iceberg and can be successful in changing some small- to medium-scale tactical issues. However, significant transformation only occurs when change occurs on a deeper level beneath the surface. Here one significant change can cause a myriad of tactical differences above the surface. We are about to look at what is beneath the surface of your iceberg. You may not like all of what you discover. Some elements of what you find may evoke strong emotion in you.

You will become conscious of things that you are currently unconscious of. If you are to unleash the power of your true potential, the first step is to become aware of what you are resonating. I believe you to be creative, resourceful and whole, in other words, you are strong, psychologically well and in a position to answer life's big questions for yourself. If you are not or do not feel ready to go beneath the surface, please stop reading now.

We are about to go deep.

Over the subsequent chapters you may decide to change your life.

The Big Picture Part 1: Your Past Life Story

To understand your iceberg and what it is resonating, you need to be aware of what makes it up beneath the surface. You can do this by creating a 'Life Story'. Capture important people and events in your life on a sheet of paper in word, picture or object form and order them in a way that makes sense to you. There will be both 'positive' and 'negative' events. They can be big or small. It does not matter. What matters is that they stick in your mind. You may not even know why they are memorable – that is fine too, just physically capture them in some form. All of these things will have one thing in common – that they have contributed significantly to you becoming the person you are today. They may have impacted on decisions you have made or shaped the things you now value most in life.

For example, in my life story I capture a time at school when I was ignored by my friends over a period of several months. I saw this as a very difficult time for me and a significant one in my teenage years as I was developing my sense of self. It had a big impact. Also in my life story is an old lady I merely caught a glimpse of as I was interviewing Indonesian villagers. She was walking up an incredibly steep volcanic slope with an enormous bundle of wood on her back. It was so large that it dwarfed her tiny frame and bent her double. It was a split second in my life, I never spoke to her, I don't know who she was, but it somehow seemed important, so I captured it.

I have coached many people through their life stories and one thing that stands out is that no one so far has had an idyllic childhood. To a greater or lesser extent, we have all had challenges to overcome. Most people go further than that and have had some kind of defining negative experience. I guess this is part of growing up and is a natural stage in the journey of human life. We are all related and so it seems as though we all go through this childhood initiation, although of course no two people's are the same.

Completing this exercise takes some reflection time that the modern world paradigm would prefer us not to take. I suggest you create an hour without interruptions initially and see where you get to. You may choose to come back to it several times over a few weeks as more thoughts and memories emerge. Once you have captured the important people and events we will look at how to interpret it in the next section.

If you want to unleash the power of your true potential and you feel that you are ready, complete and reflect on your life story before reading on.

The Meaning Behind the Story

We are now going to enter into a section that acts as a guide to interpreting your past life story. Bear in mind that different people may experience the same event and draw very different conclusions from it. That is natural. No one has a monopoly on the truth. No one is right, no one is wrong. You just have different and entirely unique perspectives and that is fine. As Susan Scott puts it in *Fierce Conversations*, 'You each own a slice of reality.'[15] Understanding this and living it at level 3 awareness can be a hugely liberating experience.

The questions that this book is about to pose are some of life's big questions. They are questions many people never take time to answer. Often people are scared about what they might come up with. Of course it is the ego that is scared. It is scared of admitting some things and wants to pretend that everything is fine as it is. The ego feels safe with the status quo.

I don't think you would have made it to this point in the book unless your soul knew that you could unleash more of its power.

As you answer the following questions you have a choice about what level you want to go to. If you want to unleash the power of your true potential you need to answer these questions from the deepest level; from the heart.

As far as we are aware, we can only be sure that we lead one life and you are in it now.

Listen to your soul.

Be honest.

Think big.

This is it.

There are many implications of past experience, but we are going to consider some of the key elements such as values, motivators and beliefs.

Your Inner Compass of Core Values

'Values' are our guiding principles, the qualities upon which we place great importance. In times of trouble and uncertainty, when you feel as if you are a small boat in rough seas, values can act as your inner compass, guiding you as you make the decisions that will get you safely through the storm.

Values can be things like freedom, variety, safety, adventure, power, love, fun, integrity, choice, flexibility, fairness, change, money, family, happiness, quality of life, the outdoors, physical activity, solitude, winning, intelligence, personal development, imagination, loyalty or control. They are by no means limited to these. In fact anything that you place a great importance on that influences how you make decisions is a value to you. You can have a value that no one else has. That is fine.

If we create a life that honours our values we tend to feel happy, fulfilled and at peace. If we ignore our values or create a life which is fundamentally at odds with them, this creates a tension deep within us that makes us feel unhappy and unfulfilled.

- *Look at the memorable events and times that make up your life story and consider the ones that stick out as the most positive and enjoyable of your life so far. These could be called 'peak' experiences. What values are you honouring in those experiences?*
- *Now look at your most difficult times. What values were not being honoured?*

For example, on my life map my travels stick out as peak experiences for me. The key values that drop out of these for me are around freedom (to travel the world), flexibility (to make up the itinerary along the way), variety (all those different cultures and landscapes), oneness (the deep similarities of all people and the help that complete strangers in foreign lands have shown me), appreciation for what I've got (clean running water, electricity, security) and open-mindedness (to accept and learn from different ways of life).

Make a list of the values that drop out of the most positive events on your life story. Once you have done this consider the following:

- *Which values appear repeatedly?*
- *Which ones resonate with you the most?*
- *Which ones are missing? Add them to the list.*
- *Make a league table of your top ten values. What is your number one value, the one you could not live without?*
- *How does this list of values inform and guide the way you live your life?*

- *Which of these values are you currently living in tune with?*
- *Which values are you currently not living in tune with?*
- *What do you know that you value, but currently you find yourself not honouring?*
- *Why is this?*
- *What could you do within the next month to bring more of this back into your life?*
- *As you consider your list of values, what are you surprised is not on it?*

Your values are not the same as anyone else's. If you look at the answers you have just captured, it is unlikely that anyone else's in the whole world would be exactly the same. On the one hand you are unique, but on the other hand everyone has values.

Values point towards the soul. They provide you with a deeper sense of direction. Living in alignment with them helps you to navigate your way along life's often difficult road. Living in alignment with them means working with the grain of your soul. Living in alignment with them means that the outward representation of your self (your ego) is resonating in tune with the inward representation of your self (your soul).

If you can live your values at level 3 awareness, you will naturally become more authentic. You will begin to resonate with a more powerful frequency in the world. People will sit up and take note. They will be more influenced by you as the strength of your actions comes from a different place; a deeper place of more power. You take a step up. You begin to invoke your two-million-bit processor in your daily life.

When I translated my life map I considered that old lady carrying the sticks. The phrase that came to mind was, 'Never let me say I've had a hard day'. It pointed to a key value of mine which is to appreciate your position within the oneness of the world. No matter how tough things get for me, I will not have to carry a huge bundle of branches up a forty-five degree volcano every day of my life and well into old age.

I don't feel guilty about this. It just is. I don't want to be one of those people who says, 'I didn't appreciate what I'd got until I lost it.' You hear those stories every day. I don't need to learn that lesson the hard way. Every day I honour this key value. I tell my wife and kids that I love them . . . and I mean it.

One of the most significant revelations of my personal life map was the very real presence of unconditional love during my childhood. I thought this was normal, but I now see that it was a huge gift that has given me confidence and a solid basis on which to build the rest of my life. I now hugely value something that I thought was just normal. Now that I am aware of it and value it, I am better placed to ensure that I truly live it at level 3 with my children.

That is priceless.

The Big M: Motivation

Companies pay thousands of pounds for motivational speakers and most leaders I coach are keen to increase their ability to 'motivate the troops'. The reason that motivation is so important is the astonishing effect it can have on people's effectiveness.

Employee A is demotivated. He slouches around doing only what he is asked to do. He doesn't go the extra mile, he doesn't drive the organisation forward, he operates well below his potential and he costs a certain amount in terms of salary. He is unhappy.

Employee B has exactly the same skills and knowledge as employee A, but is highly motivated. He is happy, does all he can, constantly looks for better ways to get things done and his approach is somehow infectious to those around him. He costs the organisation exactly the same amount of money.

Which one are you?

If you feel that you are more like employee A, how much more of your life are you prepared to spend like this? I suspect you aren't doing yourself or the organisation you work for much good in this frame of mind.

Employees cost a lot of money. In today's modern world, businesses can't afford to have high cost assets not fulfilling their potential. But what makes the difference? If you could answer that question and give people a step by step guide, you could make a huge difference to people's motivation and therefore happiness. The problem is that (just like values) what motivates people is different for everyone. What motivates you might not motivate me.

Some people are motivated by completing something that they set out to do. I am not. I am motivated by having an adventure. I'm not right, they are not wrong. We are just different and that is fine.

Motivation is crucial to the unlocking of human potential. It is seen as a huge conundrum by companies. This is mainly because they don't ask and they don't listen. If you want to motivate someone, the recipe is simple. Find out what gets them out of bed in the morning and work out between you how you can get more of that into their working lives.

It has to be a partnership.

So let's start with you.

- *What gets you out of bed in the morning?*
- *What things motivate you to put energy into your life?*

Motivators include things like having an adventure, finishing a project, getting rich, recognition, problem solving, doing a good job and making a difference to people. Anything can be a motivator and it will come as no surprise to you that they are often linked to your values.

- *Look at your life story. When were the times when you felt most motivated?*
- *What were the general themes about these times that were so motivating for you?*

When you have captured these, you have a clearer idea of your personal motivators.

- *What is your number one motivator?*
- *Out of ten, how much of that is there in your life at the moment (0 = none, 10 = my life is overflowing with it)?*
- *What could you do to increase your score by 1?*
- *Who else knows that this is your number one motivator?*
- *Who is the person who doesn't know, but if they did would be well placed to help you get more of it into your life and increase your score?*
- *What will you do about that over the next week?*

There is a huge misconception that everyone's main motivator is money. I have performed an exercise in many different organisations where people select their number one motivator. In the hundreds of people that I have taken through this only about two per cent have chosen 'getting rich' as their main motivator. Money is an important hygiene factor, but contrary to popular belief it is not a huge *motivator*. Sure it makes a difference, but the modern world paradigm overplays the importance of it. We need to get it back in balance.

Companies don't seem prepared to engage every employee one-on-one to check out what motivates them and then create more of that in their life. I suppose they think it would be too complicated and too much like hard work. They do however pay everyone. A simpler broad brush approach is to attempt to motivate people through money, but this has mixed results. If it were true that money was the greatest motivator, then the most motivated employees would be those at the top of the organisation who were paid the most money. As I am sure you will agree, this is not always the case.

The ego may crave money and the objects that it can buy,

but the soul does not. The soul is your powerful two-million-bit processor. Far more effective to engage that as your main motivated workhorse, than the relatively weak seven-bit ego! Place too much value on money and you increase the likelihood that you will remain in the ego trap.

The Secret to Happiness

If you put your values and motivators first and align your life to live with the grain of them, then you are likely to be happier as a result. Your personal effectiveness is likely to increase because you are genuinely enjoying yourself. You will be sending out strong, positive resonance in the zero point field so you will start to load life's dice. You will have a happier, more fulfilling life. You may earn less money doing what you love, but you are likely to be happier and more fulfilled.

Which is more important to you? On your death bed, as you review your life will you be more interested in the amount of money you earned over the years or the amount of happiness and fulfilment that was present in your life?

Most countries gauge their development through measures such as Gross Domestic Product (GDP). Indicators like this are purely economic measures based on factors such as material production and consumption. Traditionally, the higher these are, the 'better off' we are all supposed to be. But that is not always the case is it? Bhutan famously decided that rather than focusing solely on material measures, it would build an economy to serve its culture, including Buddhist spiritual values. As a result it measures Gross National Happiness.

How strong do you think the link is between Gross Domestic Product and Gross National Happiness?

Which country do you think has the highest GDP of all developed (OECD) countries?

I'm sure you guessed correctly. It is of course the USA with all its mental health issues.

Money is not guaranteed to bring you happiness. However it is possible for happiness to bring more money. If you do what you enjoy, you are likely to be good at it and people will want to pay for that. Maybe not immediately, but over time ... an increase in wealth can be a pleasant by-product of doing what you love. The point is that it is not the main reason.

Calibration

This is a 'being' thing, so it is difficult to calibrate 'how much' you are living with the grain of your soul. Specific measurement is an egoic response to something anyway, but here are personal examples that may illuminate where you currently stand.

I held a national training role in Australia and greatly enjoyed pulling together the international best practice of the multinational corporation that I worked for. I developed a leadership programme for the country's managers and rolled it out across the country. This role scored a hit with a lot of my values and motivators. One of my values is pragmatism. There is much in the world that sounds good, there are many new ideas and theories that people latch onto, but in my experience not a lot of it actually works in the real world. Leadership training and coaching seemed to be where I wanted to go, but I could not do it without putting it into practice and seeing that it pragmatically worked.

An opening to lead a cross-functional team in the UK arose. It was a perfect opportunity to put all the theory into practice and see what worked, so I took it. It was a large team of 100, mostly sales people and managers, that had received a varying quality of leadership over the years. Some felt lost, others abused and this area of the business had missed its targets for five years running.

The first eight months were 'hard work'. By this I mean long hours, driving and supporting people through change, managing some people up to the required standard and other people out as they were not fit for role. During this time I also became a dad, with all the stresses and strains that that brings.

My overarching purpose at this point was to prove that the 'right' way of doing things would both motivate people and hit business targets. I believed that I could make a positive difference to people's work lives and it would be beneficial for the company too. What I was trying to do was in line with my values. It felt close to my soul. As a result it did not really feel like hard work.

I remember on one occasion the alarm went off at 5am after I had managed to have only one hour's sleep. I had a choice to go back to bed or to go and catch the train in order to do some work with one of my managers with whom I had spent little time. I could have easily phoned and got out of the meeting, but I chose to go. This is a bit of the energy and power that you get from living in tune with your values.

Here were the headline results after 18 months in role:

- *A manager whom I had to manage out, thanked me as he had been miserable in his role and suddenly he 'felt free' as if a great weight had been lifted from him.*
- *We began to implement some cutting-edge systems and processes that were to my knowledge a world first.*
- *We hit our multi-million-pound sales target for the first time in five years.*
- *I received a business award.*

Now let's see what happens when you ignore your soul and don't honour your values.

We bought another company and integrated their sales team with mine. This would mean I would either be squeezed up or squeezed down. It was the latter. As a result I decided that to keep my career on track I would seek a move, but as I had been in Australia and out of the office for most of the time, key stake-holders did not know enough about me. I also had a gap in my

CV; my nemesis role. The one I had, to a certain extent, fled to Australia to avoid. If I did not take a step back and tick off this purely commercial role, my career at this company was going to be limited.

So I took it. I went from leading a team of a hundred people I cared about to leading no one. I went from coaching people (which I loved) to head to head negotiating (which I disliked). I went from living and breathing my values and being close to the right path for me to compromising my values and moving away from my path to a fulfilling life.

I could do the job. I had my end of year review and it was OK. That wasn't the issue. The issue was what it was taking out of me. I struggled to get out of bed even after eight hours' unbroken sleep because I wasn't motivated. I felt confused and unclear about what I was doing because I was not honouring my personal values. I did not feel confident. I received no pleasure from the type of business wins that other people came back to the office delighted about. I realised that I got more satisfaction from enabling other people to succeed in business than I did from doing it myself.

In retrospect I can see that I was working against the grain. Although most people said that the role was 'easier' in many ways than the previous one I had, it felt much harder to me. I could not understand why I felt so different to others in the same role. The job exhausted me in a way that far exceeded the actual quantity of work I was doing. Every now and then a thought would pop into my head, 'You could just walk out of here'. I didn't know it then, but I was taking out an overdraft on myself and one that I would soon pay for.

I went to Africa for a week on holiday and lived fully in line with my values. We camped in the wilderness and reconnected with the oneness of life on earth. In Africa what's important in life seemed so clear to me. I returned. The first day back I just could not get going. I stared blankly at the computer screen. I went to the car park and sat in my car. I cried. I went back into the office to try again. The voice in my head said, 'Get out' and this time I obeyed. Little did I know as I walked out of the doors that I would never return.

At home I just felt down. I felt lost. I didn't know what to do next. I just kept crying. My wife was concerned and persuaded me to see a doctor. I couldn't understand why, but I agreed to go (more to put her mind at rest than for me). The doctor listened to the story and signed me off work for six weeks. He said I was suffering from depression.

I was stunned.

I had always been one of the positive ones. I was always happy. I was up for anything and felt great about life. I had a successful career with what I consider to be one of the world's truly great multinational companies. How on earth had I got here? I felt tired all day, but found it difficult to sleep at night. I couldn't make decisions. I floundered around for weeks trying to 'snap out of it', but nothing worked.

I had gone from living with the grain of my values and invoking strong resonating power in my life to living against the grain and being on the receiving end of dissonating negative energy. I had gone from what at the time felt like the top of the top to what felt like the bottom of the bottom in the space of a year and I hadn't seen it coming.

At the time I could not see how life could have been much better than the good times, but I had no idea how life was about to change. My life was about to be transformed for the better in a way I could never have imagined possible, but more of that later. For now calibrate how much you think you live in line with your values. At which end of the scale are you?

I was weak. I knew I was not living in alignment with my soul, but I brushed it under the carpet and I made unacceptable compromises. You could be strong. If you are living out of tune you could make a proactive decision. That is my personal aim for the future; to proactively and honestly appraise my life regularly so that I don't go over the edge again.

As I write this, the term 'credit crunch' is used in many headlines. This is the situation that the financial market finds itself in after the large overdrafts given out irresponsibly have come back to bite them. They took out an overdraft that later came home to roost. On a personal level I experienced a 'soul crunch'. The overdraft I was taking out against my soul became too great and eventually bit back. It was nature's way of redressing the balance.

Up until now we have focused on increasing self-awareness of the factors that point to what your soul wants to resonate. These act as important guides as you progress on the journey of your life. Now we will look at something that reveals more about the ego that has been plastered on top of it. We need to understand it if we are to ask it to step aside and enable us to tap into the power of our true potential.

Rules, Rules, Rules

Look over your life story. Your ego has been using these events to build up a picture of itself. It begins by trying to work out how to operate successfully in the modern world and along the way acts to protect your vulnerable soul; the heart of you that shone forth when you first entered the world.

To find their way in the modern world, children look to compartmentalise in an effort to understand and survive in the outer world. To aid the sorting procedure, rules are created. This is a natural part of growing up and the modern world encourages the overly simplistic, if-x-then-y view of the world. Usually as we get older our view matures and we appreciate the grey areas in between this unnatural binary approach.

Not only this, but society imposes rules on us. I'm not talking about the more explicit laws that enable us to live in a civilised society, I'm talking about the more subtle 'rules' made by the ego society in which we currently live. Look out for when society or duty says that you 'should' or 'ought' to do something. This is a great way to reduce your power. Here's a challenge: next time society suggests that 'You ought to ...', don't do it. Instead do what 'You want to ...' at a deep level. See what the difference is between the two.

Remember these rules are created by a society that is currently living an unsustainable lifestyle. We talk so much about our unsustainable lifestyle that I think we become blinded to what it actually means. It means that if we continue living the way we do now, then we are going to kill ourselves. We will all die. We have to start breaking more 'rules' if we are to survive.

Of course many rules that we make up as children are useful, such as 'Don't touch the hob, it is hot', but some unhelpful rules usually slip through the net. These rules were usually created at a time when we needed help. They could have been created either by ourselves or by someone else. They had some use back then and possibly still do, but they can become overplayed and when they are out of balance, they hold you back.

For example when I was young I was told that I was forgetful and a rule I created to get through this time was, 'You must make a list'. That was fine and no doubt helped me to get through teenage years without forgetting things. However in later life I found myself ruled by lists. As a middle manager I would sit down in front of a long 'to do' list and plough through it all day. The things that were not completed went onto a new list and new jobs that had arisen during the day were added to it. The next day I would sit down and plough on through the new list.

At this point in my life the 'list rule' was no longer serving me well. It had become overblown in importance. I discovered that my lists were ruling my life. I often wasn't present. I just ploughed on head-down at a time when I should have been stopping to take a more strategic proactive perspective and look ahead.

There Are No Rules

Rules can also emerge later in our life. These often occur after events such as marriage, having children or retiring. As the ego subconsciously adjusts to its new definition in life, it can evoke old rules from the past that had lain dormant until that point.

Many women who used to be happy and independent become new mothers and start to live their lives by a new set of rules. 'I can't go back to work because it would damage my children', or 'I can't go away for the weekend because my family won't manage without me.' Just like my lists, these views may be helpful up to a point, but if overdone they start to hold people back from unleashing their true potential. That is the potential of the mother, the father and the children.

Made-up rules tend to hold you where you are. Made-up rules may prevent you from unleashing the power of your true potential. It is worth listening out for rules that you have made up when you are talking with people and consciously challenging them.

- *What rules do you carry around with you?*
- *When and why were they created?*
- *Do they really stand up to close scrutiny or do they fall over if you challenge them?*
- *Which ones are not helping you right now?*
- *Choose a made-up rule that you don't think is serving you particularly well. Break it. See what happens.*

If you make up and live by enough rules, they start to become more deeply ingrained in you. They start to become beliefs.

The Power and Fragility of Beliefs

Beliefs are incredibly powerful. People will kill themselves because of what they believe in. But what are they? They are not facts, although they often feel as if they are. They are not the truth, although they will often feel as if they are. They are 'only' things that we believe to be true. On the one hand they are incredibly powerful – powerful enough to drive some people to make the ultimate sacrifice. On the other hand they are also fragile – almost brittle – and can often be broken or changed surprisingly easily.

Beliefs can be positive or negative. You will hold both empowering and self-limiting beliefs about yourself and the world you live in; everyone does. You are a successful human being, so you are likely to have many empowering beliefs. These are beliefs that help you to operate in line with your true potential.

Some empowering beliefs I have are, 'As long as I do my best, that's good enough', 'I am good at connecting with people', 'Trust your intuition' and 'I have something important to say'. On current assessment, these beliefs are serving me well so I naturally keep them. They are examples that help my ego to work with the grain of my soul. They are helping me to advance on my journey.

Self-limiting beliefs are fascinating. We all have them. Often they are unconscious and we are unaware of them. But why would we have them? Why would we possibly want to carry something around with us that limits us and holds us back from fulfilling our true potential in a highly competitive world? It seems mad! There are three main reasons.

1) Ego Role Beliefs

As part of defining itself, your ego may have built up limiting beliefs around the role you play in life. Gill Edwards describes a common 'Drama Triangle', which involves a victim, persecutor and rescuer.[16] If your ego has a victim mentality, it may tend to hold beliefs that back that up like 'If something can go wrong, it probably will', 'Bad things always happen to me' or 'I don't deserve to be happy'. An ego taking on a persecutor role may hold beliefs like 'I am right', 'You are wrong' or 'There is only one way and it's my way'. An ego with a rescuer role may hold beliefs such as, 'I am a good person', 'He/she is relying on me' or 'I always help other people'. This may not seem limiting, but often these people unconsciously surround themselves with people playing out the other roles who sap their energy.

- *Which of these roles sounds most like you?*

It will be no surprise that the way victims behave and resonate tends to attract persecutors. Both egos can feed off the ensuing drama between these roles. Before long a rescuer may be sucked in too. This will back up their roles as well as providing food for the rescuer's ego. Unless individuals become conscious of these roles within them, they tend to repeat in a never-ending cycle. The beliefs surrounding the role limit them. Unless something changes it is hard to unleash the power of your true potential from this place.

Of course there are many different roles that the ego can take on and create beliefs around. These sound like, 'I am a mum therefore I believe that …' or 'I am a successful businesswoman and therefore I believe that …' Neither of these roles or the associated beliefs are inherently 'wrong', but if you strongly identify with a 'role' it is worth rigorously investigating it. Be aware of any self-limiting beliefs that you have attached to any roles you identify with.

- *What roles do you identify with?*
- *What limiting beliefs do these roles carry for you?*

2) Put-Upon Beliefs

Often beliefs are 'put on us' by someone else. As we grow up we are vulnerable to this and often these beliefs are put upon us by those closest to us such as parents. Again these can be positive – 'You are a sociable little boy' – or self-limiting – 'You are lazy'.

I believe that people are always doing their best, considering their iceberg. Despite all the things you need training and licences for, anyone can have a child and become a parent – the most responsible position of all. Parents are given little advice or training. Even advice that is given usually changes over the years. Between my first and second child, several guidelines were changed. The advice around when my parents had me was in many cases fundamentally different.

Parents do the best they can given their iceberg at that moment in time. I am doing the best I can given mine: however I'm sure that in the future my children will identify something I inadvertently 'put on them' that holds them back. All you can do is your best.

As my 'list' story makes clear, I was told 'You are forgetful' when I was young. I inadvertently adopted this as a belief and took it into my adult life. I happily told people I was forgetful. It became part of who I was. It supplied a self-definition for my ego. I forgot things and said, 'See I am forgetful. Sorry everyone!' It started to limit me, but now I am aware of it, I have been able to make progress removing it.

- *What limiting beliefs have been put upon you by other people?*

3) Beliefs That Helped Us In The Past

We also generate our own beliefs. As we journey through life, we collect information about what happens around us and use it to create beliefs about ourselves and the way the world works. Like rules, these usually supported us through difficult times in the past, but now hold us back. They are past their sell-by date.

Take for example Terry. He held a mid-level position in a leading global financial services company. At an assessment centre he performed well, but seemed reluctant to take on a leadership role. In a subsequent coaching discussion it emerged that he didn't want to stand out from the crowd. The conversation went something like this:

'Where does that come from?'
'I don't know.' Then after some silence a laugh, 'I don't know if it comes from school.'
'How did not standing out in the crowd serve you then?'
'Well I was bright, but small for my age. I used to get picked on in the playground. As a result I tried to fade into the background. It was a playground survival technique.'

During the following discussion it emerged that he had almost failed his university degree, but at the last minute had pulled off a first – an incredible feat. We uncovered that he had a self-limiting belief of 'If I stand out I will be attacked' and this continued through to the present day.

'How appropriate is that belief now given that you are no longer in the playground?'
'Not at all.'
'What is the implication if you continue with this belief?'
'I will not achieve what I want in my career.'

* *Consider the events in your past life story. What beliefs have you picked up along the way?*
* *Which do you see as enabling?*
* *Which ones are self-limiting?*

Some beliefs may appear to be enabling on the surface, but if they are overdone, they become limiting. A common example is 'I am a perfectionist'. Whilst 'I do a good job and get things right first time' could be an enabling and useful belief to hold, if it is overdone it can transform into, 'Unless what I have done is absolutely perfect, then I have no worth'. This can generate obsessive behaviour above the surface of the iceberg and can significantly hold people back from unleashing the power of their true potential.

- *Which of your apparently enabling beliefs do you suspect you tend to overdo?*
- *When that happens, what does it cost you?*

All beliefs tend to attract more of what they focus on. Here's how.

The Self-fulfilling Prophecy of Beliefs

Beliefs act in a self-fulfilling cycle: Belief, Feeling, Behaviour, Result. Take for example the boy who 'would probably mess it up'. During a leadership programme for sixth formers he volunteered to work through this self-limiting belief and the conversation went as follows:

'How does the belief that "you will probably mess up" make you feel?'
He looked at the desk in front of him and fidgeted nervously, 'Er ... it ... er ... makes me feel er ... no good. I feel like ... er ... I can't get anything er ... right ... er people don't er ... understand me and er ... it's all my er ... fault.'
'What behaviour does that drive in you?'
'I don't er ... get er ... the erm ... point over and er ... I er ... shy away. I er ... don't want to er ... take on er ... a role. I erm ... I guess I am er ... reluctant and er ... not very clear.'
'What result does that tend to generate?'
'Er ...' an awkward smile and then looking down at the desk again, 'things er ... tend to er ... go wrong.'

He demonstrated how the cycle worked perfectly. The belief that he would probably mess it up invoked a serious lack of self-confidence. This caused him to stammer and communicate poorly. As a result things often went wrong and this backed up his self-limiting belief that he would probably mess up. The cycle repeated over and over until this seemed to be an integral part of who he was.

Crushing Self-limiting Beliefs

The boy who would probably mess up was then asked to come up with the opposite of his self-limiting belief. This was 'I will get it right first time'. He took a moment to put on the metaphorical jacket of this belief – just for fun. Then the conversation went like this:

'How does this alternative belief make you feel?'
He took a deep breath and looked up from the desk, 'I feel confident and calm. Like it is all going to be OK.'
'How will you behave from this place?'
He smiled. 'No worries, no problem. I will talk to people and they will do the right thing.'
'What do you think the result will be?'
'Well it goes right first time.'

Not only had he communicated the stages of the opposite belief – a much more enabling one – but he had adopted it right in front of us. His language had become more positive. He lost his stutter. He communicated clearly. Acting from this place he generated just as much evidence to support his new enabling belief as he had to back up his self-limiting belief.

The boy who would probably mess up became the boy who would be a strong, successful leader before our very eyes. In a matter of minutes. The classroom was stunned.

So is the nature of beliefs. On the one hand powerful; on the other fragile.

Of course you have to want to change. Often self-limiting beliefs give you something or you would not continue to hold them. Going back to Terry, he realised that hiding away from his true potential was a habit he had got into. He was not particularly comfortable in front of other people and maintaining his self-limiting belief saved him from having to take on some difficult challenges. However carrying around this belief clearly cost him something too. He was not going to become a Finance Director if he continued to behave in this way.

Something had to give. He could either keep the belief or keep the vision of what he wanted to become. He could not keep both. They were mutually exclusive. He sighed as we looked at his vision for the future.

'It's got to go. I don't need it any more,' he said. There was an emotional quality to these words. It was as if he was saying goodbye to a childhood friend who had helped him through a time of crisis. Rather than detesting self-limiting beliefs and resisting them, it can be more effective to acknowledge them, thank them even for their help during a difficult time and politely, but firmly, say goodbye. This can be emotional. It can feel as if a bit of you is dying and in a way it is. A bit of the ego that is getting in the way of you unleashing the power of your true potential falls by the wayside. That is an integral part of the journey.

Terry was subsequently promoted. He was selected for the organisation's talent programme. I have seen his name in the paper. People in the organisation know and respect him. He is often cited as one of the company's brightest young stars. He is now well on the way to fulfilling his vision.

- *What is the self-limiting belief that most holds you back?*
- *Where does it come from?*
- *How relevant is it to the life you live now?*

Map out the 'Belief, Feeling, Behaviour, Result' format in a circle (see below), showing how the result feeds the belief, making it a self-fulfilling prophecy.

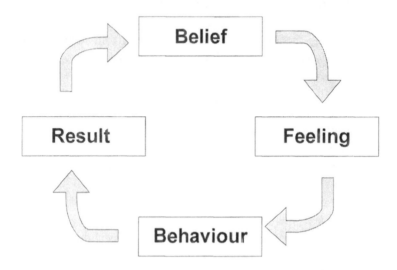

Write down the opposite of your self-limiting belief. This is likely to sound ridiculous to you. It needs to be the opposite, not a slightly better version of the self-limiting one. Shut your eyes. Imagine how the world would be if you truly believed this. Fill out the cycle again from this place.

When you have finished, you could hold a quiet memorial service for the old self-limiting belief. Thank it for its help. Acknowledge it. Then say goodbye.

As you start to build your new enabling belief into your life it can help to constantly remind yourself of it. What can you do/wear to remind you and keep this new belief fresh in your mind during the early days whilst you build up evidence to support it? I have a stone in my pocket right now for this reason. Every time I reach into my pocket I think, 'What's this?' and it reminds me. I have put my watch on my other wrist in the past and had a picture at my desk. Find something that works for you.

The good news is that there is a 'recency effect' when you

tackle self-limiting beliefs. When radio stations ask listeners to vote for the 'Top 100 songs of all time', recent songs often feature higher than older classics. So it is with your subconscious; recent evidence is given more value than old evidence. You don't have to amass as much evidence to tip the scales the opposite way in favour of the new belief. I have seen people give up a self-limiting belief very easily and quickly in a matter of days, immediately unleashing more of the power of their true potential.

If you believe it will be easy to crush your self-limiting beliefs you will be proved right. If on the other hand you believe it will be difficult, you will of course also be proved right. Such is the way of beliefs.

Over to you.

The Power and Ease of Perspectives

Here's a conundrum. On holiday two young brothers with a little sunburn take a shower. When the younger one has finished the dad dries him whilst the other showers.

'Ooh that's a bit of sunburn there,' he says.

'Sorry,' says the dad.

The older boy finishes and whilst capable of drying himself wants his dad to dry him too. The dad obliges, although quite frankly he has had enough of ablutions and wants to relax. The older boy wants to test things and pretends to be sunburnt where the dad is drying.

'Ooh that's a bit of sunburn there,' he says.

The dad is now frustrated with a job he shouldn't have to do anyway. 'Oh stop complaining,' he says.

A heartfelt argument ensues between the two.

The older boy sees this event as a demonstration that his dad does not love him as much as his younger brother. The dad sees this as an annoying event that was completely manufactured by the older boy. The younger boy sees this as a good demonstration of why you should avoid conflict.

Same event. Three different translations. Which one is right?

You will have a view based on your iceberg. The real answer is that it doesn't matter. All three are purely translations of the event that are dependent on the relative perspectives that the event is seen from. You have a choice when it comes to the perspective you take on life. You have a choice as to how you decide to 'translate' the events in your life story. Of course you cannot change the events themselves, but you can change the interpretation.

Twin boys were raised by a drunken and abusive father who spent much of his time in and out of jail. Later in life one had become successful with a good job and a stable home life. The other had mirrored his father. Psychologists studied them in an attempt to discover why there was such a difference given their apparently identical genetic background and experiences. They were stumped. They could not decipher what the difference was. They asked the individuals why they thought they had turned out the way they had and they both replied, 'With a dad like that, what do you expect?'

Here then was the key difference; it was purely down to the perspective they took. One had decided that with a dad like that he would inevitably head the same way. The other had decided that with a dad like that there was no way he could possibly make the same mistakes, having witnessed the pain it caused the loved ones around him. Both perspectives were proved right, much like the belief cycle we looked at earlier.

What you resist persists. It is no surprise that religions stress the importance of forgiveness. Without it, negative energy is ascribed to events of the past and they are granted power. Try as we might, we can't shift them.

Do yourself a favour.

Take an event from your life story that holds significant negative energy for you. Consider your translation of this event. Now think of the other people involved; what would their translation of the event be?

Think of someone whose opinion you trust, but is completely neutral in this situation. If they were presented with this situation, but not told the names of the people involved, what do you think their translation would be?

Imagine a completely separate being that had full knowledge of both the people involved and had complete knowledge of their icebergs. What would their considered opinion be?

- *You have a choice. Which interpretation will you adopt?*
- *What will this perspective give you?*
- *What will it cost you?*
- *When you deeply forgive the event on a soul level, what happens to the energy around the event?*

Some people find it hard to grasp how you can change your perspective. 'But I am the same person!' their ego cries. 'How can I change my perspective?' Actually you are not the same person. Your body is made up of different elements, about 70% of which is water. The molecules that you consisted of years ago have passed through your body and are long gone. Cells have died and new ones have rejuvenated. You are made up of different molecules today. You are literally a different person.

Different parts of the body replace at different rates, but scientists estimate that an average adult goes through a cycle of shedding and growing new cells about every 7 years. You literally have different eyes to see the world through. The old eyes that saw things in the past are not made up of the same cells as the eyes looking at these words now. Don't tell me you can't change the perspective you see through them. What a perfect opportunity to see something new.

Personal Evolution

Your life constantly evolves and so do these tasks. You may revisit your work at a later date and see events with more clarity or a different perspective. I know that I have done this.

My dad used to frequently come home frustrated by his job and would get cross easily. I took an enabling belief from this experience, 'Life's too short, chill out!'

However at a later date whilst going through a self-development session it emerged that I had suppressed my anger as a result. This was preventing me from releasing my anger and was having a knock-on effect. I realised that I was not fully experiencing life's emotions. I was not living the true rainbow of life. Although I was somewhat reticent, I worked on feeling anger when it arose in me and being honest to it, letting it out rather than suppressing it. To my surprise as a result I started to feel positive emotions more deeply too. So my translation of this one event has changed over time and no doubt yours will too.

Clearly as you progress through life more events appear on your past life story. As you work on crushing your self-limiting beliefs and altering your perspective, the translation changes. At different points in your life, different values and motivators will come to the surface. What turns me on today is different to what turned me on when I was twenty, which is different to when I was five. Otherwise I would still love nothing more than playing with Lego. This is natural.

It is worth sparing a thought for the people that feature in your life story. I recently worked with a client whose sister had gone through a lot of this kind of personal awareness work and had 'taken it out' on the people that featured in her life story.

This is not a necessary part of the process.

You don't have to address everything with other people. This is not about them, it's about you. Remember it's your personal journey.

So far we have only considered half of your personal journey. Now we are going to complete the story.

The Big Picture Part 2: Your Future Life Story

I have some sad and perhaps shocking news for you. You are going to die. Sooner or later you are going to die. There is no escape. You are made up predominantly of molecules of water and one day those molecules will be free to play in the lakes and streams again. You will fall as rain, you will water plants and animals, you will trickle down streams and travel the oceans. Maybe a bit of the essence of you will stay with these molecules. I hope so. Death is no bad thing.

We in the Western world don't talk about death much. We seem to see it as a taboo subject. We live in denial of what true contemplation of our ultimate passing will cause in us. Our ego is fearful. It thinks that if we all realise on a deep level that we will all ultimately die, there will be anarchy. It thinks that it will cease to exist. On a deeper level our soul knows this is not the case and is not afraid.

The average life expectancy in the Western world is about 80 years. You may live longer, you may live shorter. That is down to life's dice. Compare how many years you have lived so far to how many years you expect to live for.

- *What percentage of your life have you already lived?*
- *How many more years are there until you expect your death to occur? I want you to picture the scene at your funeral.*
- *Mourners will gather. Who will be there?*
- *Imagine being able to eavesdrop on conversations between people. What would you like them to be saying about you?*
- *Someone will no doubt take the stage to read out your eulogy. Who will it be?*
- *What will they say?*
- *What will you have achieved in your life?*
- *How will you be remembered?*

- *What will your impact have been on other people?*
- *What will you have stood for?*
- *What legacy will you have left?*

If you are about half way through your life, you will have already written half of your obituary. It will emanate from your past life story. Take a look at your past life story. How closely does it match what you want people to be saying at your funeral?

- *What are the key things that are missing?*
- *What could you do to bring these into your life so that you stand a chance of achieving what you want your life to stand for?*

As far as we can be sure, we only have one life. You will only ever get to live this day (today) once. This is it. What will you do with it?

Your life is like a play. You get to write in the scenes and the actors through your actions.

- *If you were writing the next scene, what would you make happen?*
- *Which character would exit stage left, not to re-appear?*
- *Which one would enter stage right?*

Good script. Now the big question:

- *How well will you act it out?*

Consider your values and your motivators. Start a fresh page in your notebook and start to piece together some of the things you would love to do in your life. These may be small tactical things that appear on 'life lists' such as swimming with dolphins or could be broader things like 'running my own business'. You may have very specific milestones such as 'I want to work for a charity for a year before I am fifty' or you may have no idea. You may find it difficult to think beyond a couple of years. Of course that's OK. Just like your past life story, this is a process that is revisited, amended and updated throughout your life.

Start to piece them together. Literally write the script of your life. Don't get hung up on getting this 'right' first time. You could produce several options of future life stories and then reflect on which one you most like the sound of.

- *What one thing would achieve a significant proportion of your future life events?*
- *What can you do today to begin to set that up for the future?*

As you live your future life story, the events and milestones move from your future life story to your past life story. As you grow older you will have achieved more, you will have less to do. You could see that as positive (you have achieved the things you wanted to do in your life) or negative (you are running out of time). Of course this is a merely a perspective and so you can choose the one that serves you best.

Your future life story constantly evolves as do you. Things happen earlier than expected, things 'get in the way', things change. That's fine, add these unexpected events to your past life story and edit your future life story accordingly.

It is amazing to think that people may have a clear agenda for a one-hour business meeting to ensure that the discussion stays on track, but no agenda for their life to ensure that stays on track. Without a clear plan we run a higher risk of 'waking up' one day and realising with shock that this is not what we wanted.

I think this feeling contributes to mid-life crises. Someone experiences an event that brings into reality their mortality and they suddenly realise that they are significantly 'off track'. This can result in a huge jerk in a different direction in an attempt to catch up. I don't want to wake up one day and realise that I wasn't present for my life. It is that 'waking up' that is the act of becoming more conscious.

In 1953 a graduating class at Yale was questioned about their plans for the future. It was discovered that 84% had no goals, 13% had goals in their heads and 3% had written down goals. Twenty years later the students were tracked down again. The 3% with their goals written down were worth more in financial terms than the other 97% put together. Not only that, they had better health and enjoyed better relationships. There is something about writing it down that helps to unleash the power of your true potential.

Your future life story becomes real in the world.

It really, truly exists in some kind of format in the world.

You have a statement of intention. This enables you to invoke the power of intention

You resonate it more strongly and then a strange thing happens.

Meeting You Half Way

This chapter is a challenging one and you may have found it tough, especially if you have completed all the exercises at a deep soul level.

When you develop deep personal awareness and work through these or similar exercises you are better placed to live your values and motivators more truly. This increases the strength of what you resonate at a quantum level. People start to pick up on your increased gravitas and presence. You start to unleash the power of your true potential, the vulnerable, but profound power of your soul.

As you chip away at the unhelpful bits of the ego that have been consciously or unconsciously holding you back, you start to step out of your own way. The ego operator begins to listen to the two-million-bit processor and work with it rather than being frightened of it. You begin to invoke the power of your subconscious.

At this point a strange thing happens.

The world seems to meet you half way.

People and events that seem to carry a piece of the jigsaw start to appear in your life. This book may indeed be one of those things that appeared in your life at just the right time. There is no coincidence here. It has been attracted by your resonance. As your resonance increases in power, do not be surprised if it attracts ever more incredible events into your life that help you along the way – it is only natural. It is the law of attraction.

The problem is that if you are not listening in the right way, you can miss the assistance and opportunities that come your way as a result of what you are putting out into the zero point field. Remember that the energy that connected those separated quantum particles enabled them to 'hear' each other as well as 'talk' to each other. You are a 'receiver' as well as a 'transmitter'.

So how do you listen to the zero point field and take advantage of the inherent natural power that you are invoking?

You Are a Receiver

The One paradigm sees you as both a transmitter and a receiver within the zero point field of quantum physics. You are subtly, but irrefutably, connected to everything. The exercises in the previous chapter were designed to help you to identify your (often competing) ego and soul. With an increased depth of self-awareness you are better placed to align your ego and your soul. With less interference and internal noise, you begin to invoke the power of your soul; the power of your true potential; the self-actualisation within Maslow's hierarchy of needs. Not only that, but you can listen more easily to what's going on outside you.

Nature seeks balance, so as you resonate more power into the zero point field, it is just natural that what you receive back should also intensify.

The more you put in, the more you get out.

If you know how to listen to it, there is significant competitive advantage for you in the zero point field. This chapter describes how you can receive messages from it.

Nature is the greatest power and animals and birds have significant lessons for us here. They don't have much of an ego, if any at all. Their soul just shines forth for all to see. They just 'are'. If this is the case, then they should be good at receiving information from the zero point field.

Animal Instincts

Our ancestors used to watch and learn from animals. The ancient shamans saw that even before weather patterns would appear in the sky, animals would prepare for what was to come. They watched bears treat wounds with hemlock. In the old world, animals were the source of the shaman's wisdom and power.

However, civilised society has lost touch with the natural world. It has become so separated that it has turned everything on its head. Instead of learning from animals, we use them and disregard them.

I have been told by people that the key spiritual difference between us and the animal kingdom is that we have souls and they don't. There we go, trying to separate ourselves and make ourselves superior again. The One paradigm disagrees. We are the same. People who find this hard to accept should note that the people who decreed that animals don't have souls only decided to grant women souls in the fourteenth century (and even then by the narrow margin of just two votes). If there was a key spiritual difference between us and animals it would surely be that we are more identified with our egos than them. So what's in it for us? What could we possibly learn from animals?

Scientists have been tracking fourteen electronically tagged sharks off Florida since 2003. In 2007, they left their territory for the first time and swam to deeper water. Twelve hours later Hurricane Charlie hit the area. The sharks returned two weeks later and have remained in their normal territory since.

The 2004 Boxing Day tsunami provided many examples of strange animal behaviour in the lead up to the disaster. Fishermen reported catching twenty times the usual number of fish on the three days preceding the tsunami. Flamingos that usually bred at the Point Calimere wildlife sanctuary flew inland to higher ground. Fifty miles north of Phuket, elephants became agitated for several hours and then just before the tsunami hit the area, they broke their fetters and charged to higher ground, taking some lucky Japanese tourists with them. Although many thousands of people were killed in the tsunami, relatively few animals were killed.

There are many documented examples of animals demonstrating proactive responses to impending danger. How do they do it?

Swallows: A Lesson in Intuition

Swallows migrate from the UK to South Africa every year – that's a total of 6,000 miles. Six months later, they return and after a round trip of 12,000 miles and a break of six months, they find their way not only back to the same country, but often to exactly the same nest they used the year before. It is absolutely staggering that a bird with a brain that is half a gram in weight can complete such an amazing feat. It is even more incomprehensible when you consider that we have a brain 2,500 times heavier, but can easily become lost on comparatively short journeys ... sometimes even when we have Sat Nav! How do swallows do it?

Like many things this book discusses, the answer is not completely known, but we surmise that it is to do with *instinct*. The *Collins Dictionary* definition of instinct includes 'inborn intuitive power' and intuition is indeed the key. Intuition is defined as 'knowledge or belief obtained neither by reason nor by perception'. It is a hunch. It is unjustified. No one knows where it comes from. But it seems that if you could tap into it and you trusted it, it could take you on a 12,000-mile round trip to South Africa and back, finishing at exactly the same barn you set out from. You will no doubt appreciate the inherent power in that.

We celebrate human intuition with stories of detectives who have a 'gut feeling' or businessmen who 'follow a hunch', but when it comes down to it, big picture intuition is increasingly being squeezed out in favour of small picture facts and figures. The modern world paradigm has little space for hunches because it has no room for mistakes (remember that evolution, the most powerful force in the world, is based on making some mistakes). As a result instead of making intuitive leaps, we take a long time and work hard to make another small shuffle forward ... often in the same direction.

If you could start to understand where your intuition comes

from and how it works, there would be an immense power that you could tap into and use in your life. We know intuition exists. We value it in stories, films and legends, but we don't know exactly how it works, so we are often afraid to use it in everyday life.

Do you think you have access to the sixth sense of intuition? I think you do. I believe everyone can draw on their intuitive knowing if they can just work out how they can tap into it. You are an individual. The way you access your intuition may be different to the way I access mine. I don't believe there is a simple 5-step plan to access intuition, but there are some key blockers and some tips which can help. We will look at both.

So where does a swallow's intuition come from? There are two key possibilities.

1 The intuition is inborn in the swallow. Somewhere deep in the DNA of the sperm and egg that make up a new swallow is information that tells it how to migrate. It is just natural to the swallow.
2 The swallow listens to information in the here and now. The bird can somehow pick up on the waves of information in the zero point field and this informs the swallow what to do. It is just natural to the swallow.

I suspect it is a bit of both, but either way, this power is inherent in the natural world. It is just natural and therefore it is accessible to you too if you want to draw on its power. After all, nature is the greatest power.

Can you access your intuition? Your brain is 2,500 times bigger than a swallow's. We all come from the same source. We are all related. If swallows can, then you can. The problem seems to be that animals are somehow better at picking up on their intuition than we are. Why might that be?

Modern World Barriers

Animals don't live in the modern world. They just are. They don't have the same distractions as we do.

Scientists have noted that wild animals are better at sensing imminent danger than domesticated ones. It seems that just the mere influence of humans with their cultural systems and rules is enough to dampen down animals' inbuilt instincts. It is not out of the question to believe that we had this ability in the past, but the distractions of society and ego have covered it up.

This is dangerous. The majority of us seem to have lost access to our sixth sense – a key power that exists in the natural world. The good news is that it has not gone for ever; we just need to re-learn more consciously how to access it if we are to benefit from its inherent wisdom.

Wild animals are not subjected to the same barrage of noise that the modern world puts before us as we try to listen to the zero point field. In fact forget the zero point field, it puts significant barriers in the way of listening full stop.

There are three main sources of interference or noise that get in the way for us. If we are aware of them, we are better placed to minimise them.

Outer Noise

As discussed, the modern world has significantly separated itself from nature. One key side effect of the speed of technological development has been the amount of 'noise' that we are bombarded with.

We used to have 'quiet time' imposed on us, so we never had to protect it ourselves. Suddenly it has all disappeared, but we are not yet in the habit of protecting it, so if we are not careful, we perpetually live in a world of outer noise.

We used to be uncontactable when out of the house, but now we have mobile phones. Some people never turn them off and always answer them, no matter where they are. I saw a group of friends the other day sitting around a table in a restaurant and each of them had turned away from the table and was talking into their phone with a finger in their other ear. Little chance of listening to the others round the table. Remember that the mobile phone has only been around about five thousandths of a second on our evolutionary clock, but look at the 'noise' it creates in our lives if we are not careful.

You used to have to rely on the post, then you could receive a fax. Now email makes demands instantaneously. Portable laptops mean we are in contact in even more places and BlackBerrys mean that email has finally made it to our pockets. There is no respite.

There used to be 'quiet time'. It was also called 'dead time' when people had to stop and just be. Now we have access to hundreds of people to talk to, text or email and we have access to all our favourite tunes, films and programmes every minute of the day. We are bombarded with adverts that tell us we need more things to fit in. The noise we live in is incessant. It is always there. Even the films and programmes we watch seem to be more blatant, multicoloured and larger than life. It sometimes seems as if our minds have become so over-stimulated, that they find it hard to sense subtlety any more. It's like going to a disco and then walking out with your ears ringing. If someone talks quietly behind you, you just can't hear them.

- *When was the last time you sat in silence and did nothing?*
- *What would happen if you stopped?*

I asked a friend this recently. She looked at me with terror in her eyes,

'Oh no. I couldn't do that. That's too scary. Who knows what might happen. I'd fall to pieces.'

In a way she is spot on. If you stop, there's a chance that

the modern world paradigm and the ego-dominated world that we have all constructed may well fall to pieces in front of our very eyes. Once the dust has settled though, we may be left with an extraordinarily clear view of what we are here to do; of what it's all about.

Many people have a fear of being alone with themselves. They are out of practice and have lost touch with who they really are and what they yearn for.

Are you one of them?

Here's a challenge. Schedule some time to turn everything off. Remove all external stimulus and noise. Just sit and be. Don't consider any big life questions, don't try to work out what you are supposed to be doing, just listen to your own breathing and the silence around you.

A senior plant manager recently tried this with me. Immediately he started laughing. This was because of the second barrier.

Inner Noise

We can't have all that outer noise going on and not expect some kind of impact on our inner selves. The high levels of outer noise raise the threshold of what seems uncomfortably quiet for us internally. Our ego takes over to fill the space. The plant manager was laughing because as soon as he had tried to stop and just be, he had immediately started thinking about scheduling.

'OK, that's fine,' I said, 'just put that to one side for now and try again.'

He did. Something else popped in to his head. We kept repeating the process until he became stiller. Eventually he looked to one side and was quiet and still, possibly for the first time ever in his life. He managed 28 seconds. In that half a minute his gravitas and presence filled the room in a way that it had not done before. With a clear and still mind comes great power.

Businesses have been downsizing and stripping out costs

in repeated cycles for years. More and more is therefore expected from fewer and fewer people. Technological advances have helped to consistently increase the burden of 'doing' that has been imposed on employees. Like the proverbial camel, many of us are now bent double, straining under the weight. One by one, the straws are added as we are asked to do more, the same way. Unless we can find a different way, camels' backs break, fuelling the WHO prediction of stress and depression. We've got to find a different way.

We are way out of balance. Firstly we seem addicted to outer world noise, as if we are somehow losers if we enjoy silence for a few hours a week. Secondly even if we manage to find a quiet space, we find it difficult to switch off our minds so we sit there listening to our ego chattering away. That voice in our minds just keeps on talking. In many ways it is like a mad person on the streets spouting a constant stream of consciousness. The only difference is that it is going on inside our heads instead of out loud.

Small difference.

So what is it saying? It warns us not to do this, to remember to do that, asks what other people might think and it often worries about anything and everything. It often uses rationale to explain why things have to be the way they are. It often does not want to change. It is petrified of what we are getting into right now. Deep down it knows that there is something here that can cut off the powerful hold it has over you. It may be telling you that all this is rubbish.

The soul does not talk the language of the ego. It is silent. It just resonates. When you listen to it in the right way, you just *know*. You know at a deeper level than you could ever explain. Listening to the soul is incredibly powerful. It is the silent resonance of not only your soul, but of everyone else's too. It is the profound resonance of the zero point field.

Paradigm Noise

Along with the blatant outer noise of the modern world and the more subtle, but disturbing inner noise of our incessant thoughts, there seems to be the silent, but palpable noise of the current world paradigm itself. This is the noise that comes from the 'expectations' of people who live in the modern world.

For example, the modern world values fame. These days some people are famous simply for being famous and they often make a lot of money out of it. Someone seems to have deemed that fame equals success and we all desperately want it. If we can't have it, we follow celebrities like voyeurs. If we aren't interested we are a bit strange.

Someone seems to have deemed that everyone wants more money, a bigger house and more things. Anyone who doesn't want those things is also a bit strange. Someone has deemed that life is hard and anyone who says otherwise is a bit strange. Someone has deemed that you just can't tell people the truth. Someone has deemed that you must do what you are doing and there couldn't be any other way. Someone has deemed all sorts of things important that make up the modern world paradigm.

That 'someone' is you and me. Collectively, we are all responsible for signing up to and following the 'rules' of the modern world paradigm. Now it's time to stop, take a step back and listen.

Listening to the Zero Point Field

Often we think we are listening, when in fact we are not. For example children often talk to us when we are busy. We may say, 'Yes' and 'Oh' to them, but we are not present. Our mind is elsewhere. In truth, we often have no idea what they are talking about. In one of the companies I worked for, we recognised this – it was called an 'out'. During meetings people often said, 'I'm sorry I was on an "out", please can you repeat that.' This was an effective way to prevent nodding dog syndrome, where everyone nods, but no one has heard.

When we do listen, there are actually three levels of listening.

Level 1 listening: This is ego-dominated listening. There are two modes to this. One is listening to what your ego is saying. For example someone could be talking to you and you are actually listening to the voice within your head. This is the voice of your ego saying, 'I'm hungry' or 'This room is hot' or 'This person is boring'.

The other mode is that your ego is listening only for its next chance to speak. It is hearing what it wants to hear so that you can say something, often making links with your experiences. Do you know someone who always seems to turn the conversation around and talk about themselves? Do you know someone who you talk to regularly, but they never really 'hear' you? They are listening at level 1. As you can imagine, with level 1 listening people are not really listening to much outside of themselves, let alone the subtleties of the zero point field.

Here's an example. On a senior executive development programme a delegate was in a leadership role-play with someone acting out a poor-performing member of his team. The poor performer described their busy working week, finishing with '... and then I go home to look after my sick mum all weekend'.

'I understand,' the delegate said, moving swiftly on.

'I don't think you do,' I interjected. 'What did he just say?'

'He said he works all weekend.'

The level 1 listening in this case was so extreme, that a completely different message was heard from the one that had been given. Rather than tending to a sick mother, the executive thought he was hard at work on business cases all weekend.

The current world paradigm seems to support this

behaviour. It values talking and telling over listening and asking. This is because the current world paradigm is dominated by people like you and me who operate mainly in the ego level of Maslow's pyramid. The ego constantly needs to be noticed by others and is always seeking to build self-esteem through other people. This behaviour gets in the way of listening to other people. From this level of listening you can forget the zero point field.

Level 2 listening: This is good functional listening. This is listening not only to what the person is saying, but how they are saying it. It listens to body language as well as tone and words. When you ask how someone is and they reply, 'Fine', but their body language and tone indicate that they are far from fine, this is being able to say, 'You don't sound fine, what's up?' This is the level of listening most of us aspire to.

Really good level 2 listeners are able to pick up on some of the emotions behind the words. They are able to hear what is not being said. This excellent level of listening borders on the messages that you can pick up on in the zero point field.

Level 3 listening: This is being open to messages that are in the zero point field. Although I use the term 'listening', these messages come from beyond the 'normal' sensory capabilities of people like listening and observing. This is the proactive listening of animals sensing impending events. There are many different terms for it such as intuition, instinct or a sixth sense. It is not merely useful on your journey towards realising your highest potential – it is a vital part of the journey. The questions that will be asked of you often cannot be answered by our normal framework of reference. They are life's fundamental questions. Answering them requires more.

As you begin to tap into your intuition, be aware that others may not be ready to hear about it. Although in the past many people were valued for their gut instinct, we don't seem to trust it any more. It is reserved for famous detectives, not for the likes of you and me. As we have not exercised that muscle, it is wasting away in us. We need to practise. We need to re-train it. We need to build up our trust in it. It will serve us well if we give it a chance.

As you can imagine, there is a lot of information in the zero point field. In fact everything is in the zero point field; that is why it is so fundamentally important and why it carries such power.

To be able to tap into its power, the first step is to minimise the noise that gets in the way.

Pick a conversation that is coming up and practise minimising inner and outer noise. Listen really carefully to the other person. Immerse yourself in their life. If they get distracted from the conversation by external factors just notice it and observe.

- *What is different from this quieter place of being?*
- *What was useful for you?*
- *How could you remember to consciously generate this state again?*

Practise until this becomes a normal approach for you. Watch your relationships, understanding, rapport, empathy, influence and power grow as a result.

Once you can control the noise, there are two different ways in which you can tune in. The first is through 'undivided attention'. By this I mean totally undivided. I mean immersing yourself in the person with whom you are talking or the people you are with. The second is almost the opposite. It is by opening up completely to any messages that the zero point field may choose to send you. You open up and you let it come.

Undivided Attention

If you are in conversation with someone and you give them your pure, undivided attention, you are listening at level 2.

If you can listen with *their* ears, if you can truly immerse yourself in what it is to be them, from an open-minded place, if you can take 'you' completely out of the equation, then you may start to be able to tune into the quantum signals they are sending out.

From this place of ultimate empathy, you can hear what the deeper, inner, true self is resonating (in silence). This is the place where the individual's highest potential lies. This is their soul. This is their *true* potential; the potential that exists above the ego level on Maslow's hierarchy of needs.

The words that the ego produces are less important when you can listen at this level. In fact often, their voice tells you something repeatedly that a deeper level of awareness within you knows is not true. But the ego talks so loudly it is hard to ignore. Many people end up living incongruently with their highest true potential. In these cases, you can feel the 'dissonance' as what they say clashes with the deeper signals that their soul is transmitting. Sometimes this is heard on some kind of level by everyone except the person talking. You may know someone like this, someone whose words somehow seem empty, someone who seems to be ignoring a fundamental truth about themselves.

When you gain messages from the zero point field, it is usually silent. There is no spectacular crackle or zap! You just become aware of 'knowing' something. You may 'see' it, 'feel' it or 'hear' it, but not in the literal conscious way. It is an inner knowing that comes from a different aspect of your consciousness, not a surface level ego knowing.

Undivided attention is a true gift. When was the last time someone gave you a damn good *listening* to? When did you last do it to someone else? Once during a self-development programme I experienced a significant shift in my awareness of the One paradigm. Following this I returned home and gave my son my undivided attention, just for half an hour. It was as if I was looking into his eyes for the first time ever. I had never been aware of how beautiful and blue they were. I hadn't really, deeply *seen* them before; I'd just looked at them. He was three years old. I can recommend looking deeply into your loved ones' eyes with true undivided attention. It is a great gift to give and to receive. Don't leave it too late.

When you give someone undivided attention, the rest of the world, including yourself, seems to drop away. This can sometimes lead to a strange dream-like state where you and the other person are in a world of your own.

Let me share a few examples of undivided attention with you.

Example 1: How Are You? Really?

I asked one client how he was at the start of a leadership coaching session.

'Yeah OK,' he responded, 'I'm busy, really busy because I'm trying to hand over my current role, but I hope it will get better when I start my new job.'

The word 'hope' really grated. The 'o' in hope sounded hollow and rusty, like looking down a rusty old pipe sawn in two.

'When I join the new team,' he continued, 'I hope it will be a lot better.'

There it was again.

'That sounds like an empty hope,' I ventured.

He paused, looked at the table and sighed. After a while he looked up at me, 'Yes you're right ...' and we began to talk about what was really important. Within the first 30 seconds of the pretend 'ego' conversation we were suddenly having a Real conversation. We were onto something that his soul was crying out for.

If you truly immerse yourself in the person you are with, if you can remove your ego so that 'you' almost disappear, then from that place, you can begin to hear the messages they are sending out in the zero point field. From there you can have a Real conversation. From there lives can be changed.

Example 2: The First-Timer

Jacquie was in her first management role. As I coached her, it became clear that she was spending a lot of time frantically doing lots of small tasks and was constantly fire fighting. All the thoughts she had about her people were very tactical and small scale. I suddenly became aware that she had a great inherent ability to tap into her intuition. If she could just try it out, it would help her to stop all this frantic doing of small tasks and instead enable her to focus on the big things that mattered.

I prompted her, 'I'd like you to share with me one big intuition that you have about each of your team members. It can be as wild and whacky as you want. It won't go any further than this room. It's fine to make a mistake. I'd just like to hear what your intuition says.'

There was silence for a few seconds as she gazed out of the window giving undivided attention to each of her team members. She noticeably calmed down and it seemed as if her breath slowed. It was almost as if she went into a trance. After a while she reported back:

'1 *My pregnant team member will go on maternity leave and won't come back.*
2 *The contractor that I hope will join full time won't – when his contract is up he will leave and go travelling.*
3 *The final member of my team is not happy and will hand her notice in once the current project is finished.'*

She came back from her calm trance with a bump and looked back at me with a surprised look on her face.

'Oh my god. If that happened, my entire team would disappear at the same time in September.'

On returning to work, Jacquie had open conversations with each of her team members and they backed up her intuition. As a result of this she was able to set up a proactive plan with HR to ensure people were brought in at appropriate times to maintain continuity in her team. Her intuition saved a potentially damaging business situation.

Not bad for a first-timer.

Example 3: The Nurse

Janet finished her shift. Like all good nurses, she had given her patients undivided attention. Although all the charts and vital statistics were in order, one patient troubled her. Her intuition told her that something was not right. As she handed over to the next shift, she asked them to keep an eye on him and to check him more regularly than normal.

They did and on one such visit they found that he had stopped breathing. They were able to resuscitate him and he survived. If it had not been for the nurse following through on her intuition, he would be dead. When I discussed the One paradigm with her, she was fascinated.

'I knew it,' she said, 'I knew there was something like that,' and she linked this story directly to it.

Everyone has access to intuition. You may find it harder or easier than others to tap into yours. That is fine. If you make it safe for someone to practise tapping into the zero point field, you may be amazed at what turns up. You may have a Real conversation for the first time.

You may not. That's fine too. Remember, allowing for mistakes drives evolution, the most powerful force on earth. Either way you will develop as a result.

These are examples of what happens when you give true undivided attention to others. If you can quieten the noise of the outer and inner worlds, if your ego can step to one side just for a moment and you practise doing it, you are able to pick up on something deeper in others.

They are made up of quantum particles that are resonating, just like you are, just like everything is. If you can quell the noise that gets in the way, your particles can receive the messages that their particles are sending out. You are able to immerse your-selves in the zero point field. Your icebergs are able to 'hear' each other and converse on a deeper level. You are able to really know a little more of each other and to engage the great power that lies beneath the surface. Profound and significant change is possible from this place. Conversations that take place in this space often unleash incredible power that was only represented by potential before.

People have described this phenomenon as 'being in flow' – a dream-like state in which things seem to happen on a different level. A different type of communication between people is possible – it is as if you co-create something from a different place of being. Things are possible in this state that are outside the normal realms of our actions.

Intuition is not magical. It is not all blinding lights and spectacular visions. It is a natural, integral part of us that we have lost touch with. We are unpractised in it and do not trust it like swallows do. It is also a highly effective way of converting some of your latent 'potential' into 'reality'. Flex that muscle. Think of an opportunity to give someone your undivided attention.

- *Who is it?*
- *When will you give them your undivided attention and for how long?*

If you enter into this exercise with an aim, you will not be giving the other person undivided attention. No aim, just undivided attention.

Afterwards you may quietly reflect on the experience.

- *What did this new approach unleash in you?*
- *What did it unleash in them?*

Remember this may be your first outing – do not expect miracles. You may be out of practice in the skill of giving someone your undivided attention. Look for opportunities to build it up. See what happens as a result. Note intuitions that you receive from this place.

What Divides Our Attention?

With all the obvious benefits of giving someone undivided attention, the question has to be asked, why do we not do it? Part of it is about awareness. Now that you are aware, you may choose to behave differently to engage this approach.

Another reason is fear. Fear of what may come up if we truly engage with someone on this level. Fear of knowing someone intimately. Fear of being known. Fear of engaging your iceberg and theirs. Fear of what may result. Fear of uncovering the truth. Fear of uncovering the failings of the ego. Fear of getting it wrong. Fear of making a mistake. Fear of evolving.

Fear of having a real conversation.

What do you think would happen if you had a real conversation with your best friends about some of the ideas in this book that resonate most strongly with you? Do you have a fear of ridicule? I think you would be surprised. As I began to own the messages in this book more and more, I spoke with friends and colleagues about them. To a man, they were all engaged and interested. A real conversation ensued about some of the deeper things in life. Consistently it felt like a conversation our souls were crying out for.

I spoke with doctors, nurses, corporate directors, finance business partners, coaches, aunts, grandparents, religious people, atheists, taxi drivers, carpet business owners, the lot. Where I expected resistance, there was enthusiasm. Where I expected ridicule there was interest. All conversations were real. Everyone was present.

Because of where we are poised in history, we can no longer afford to have conversations that are not real.

Letting Come

Another way to tap into the zero point field is almost the opposite of 'undivided attention'. Rather than focusing on an individual or group, you completely open your mind and 'let come'. Of course you must clear your mind of the ego voice. Each time you hear it say something, just notice it, smile and put it to one side. It's OK to notice. If you are noticing, you are already winning.

I have never been that good at meditation. My ego keeps chatting away and thinking about things to do. I find it hard to completely clear my mind and sit in silence, but on the occasions that I have, I feel refreshed afterwards. I also feel more 'centred'; like I have a clearer view of what's important. I somehow *know* what to do next, even if I have not been specifically thinking about it. In this day and age where there is often too much to do, being able to prioritise is an increasingly important skill.

The act of prayer that has been so widespread across many cultures for centuries would seem to tap into both 'letting come' and 'undivided attention'. It is a quiet activity alone or in groups that attempts communication with a higher power. Whatever your beliefs, people must have gleaned something useful from it over the years or the practice would have died out long ago.

The best way to 'let come' is to relax and be open. Park the constant chattering of the ego, even for a short period of time. Meditation practices state that you can only clear the mind if you focus on your breathing. Each time you become aware that your mind is not on your breath in or out, then it has wandered into ego chat.

As you spend more time in the apex of human achievement, 'self-actualisation', and as you hone your intuition 'muscle' through practice, intuitive messages will come to you more frequently.

Theory U

A structure for 'letting come' is described in the book *Presence* (Peter Senge *et al.*). In it the authors describe the three stages of entering into this different place: see diagram below.[17]

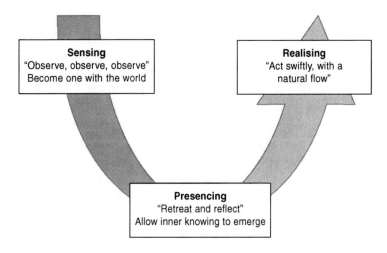

From Presence: *Human Purpose and the Field of the Future.* Peter Senge, C. Otto Scharmer, Joseph Jaworski, Betty Sue Flowers (Nicholas Brealey Publishing)

1) Sensing

Here at the top left corner of the 'U' we are encouraged to 'Observe, observe, observe'. In becoming as one with the situation and fully opening our minds to what may be, we are able to really 'tune in' to the frequency of zero point field resonance. Undivided attention lives here.

2) Presencing

Here we retreat and reflect, descending to the bottom of the 'U' to 'Let come'. We employ not only an open mind, but an open heart and an open will. What will be will be. We take a half step back from the world, we step back from the edge of life and somehow that enables us to listen at a different level. It is as though we can hear the future that is seeking to emerge through our actions.

3) Realising

Once we have presenced, we move up the right hand side of the 'U' and 'Act swiftly' on the knowing we have received, 'with a natural flow'. Actions resulting from this place tend to have more gravitas and more 'presence' about them. This is an important and a powerful approach for authentic leaders if they expect others to be inspired by their actions and follow them.

In today's modern world we are encouraged to shoot across the top of the 'U'. Busy, busy, busy. Something happens and we must react immediately. Little thought time or reflection goes into the decision. Indeed the authors of Theory U describe the approach as the 'blind spot of our time'.

Alternatively, the opposite danger is that people reflect too much. They immerse themselves in the situation, but do not act. Often self-limiting beliefs emerge – 'I can't do anything about this', or 'They will laugh at me' – and this prevents what has the potential to be an influential conversation.

There's that potential again. How are we going to actualise it if we don't commit to going through the whole 'U'?

Hearing the Messages

As you descend into the 'U' and 'let come', you may be surprised by some of the messages or intuitions that come to you. If you are listening at level 3, you may hear useful messages that come from a different place than normal. You are able to tap into the two-million-bit processor of your unconscious mind and receive messages from the zero point field.

Like all these things, the first time may be hard as you are unpractised and may not know what you are meant to be 'hearing'. Here then are the key mediums through which intuitive messages from the zero point field may arrive in your consciousness.

Voice

I ignored my intuition for years. When I finally started listening to it, I realised it had been there all along. For me it was sometimes a very quiet voice – a small thought at the back of my mind. For example, when I was 'stuck' in the job that was the antithesis of what I wanted to spend my life doing, I had some very bad days and sometimes specific events within those days would really knock me. On more than one occasion a little voice at the back of my mind quietly said, 'You could just walk out'.

I can still remember hearing one of these instances specifically as I stood next to the office printer. I went hot and something whispered in my mind, 'You could just walk out'. It came from a different place to the constant chattering voice in my mind. I can appreciate the subtlety of that now, but I didn't then. I didn't listen. That was a few months before I went down.

Knowing

'What's your new year's resolution?' I asked
  'To go to Australia,' my friend replied.
  'Forever or for a holiday?'
  'I don't know. Somewhere between the two,' she said, 'maybe for a few years.'
  At that moment I knew that I would go with her.

This 'knowing' shocked me. It was strange. Consider the feeling you get when you know something and apply it to the following situation: I had a good job that I enjoyed, lots of friends close by and I was living with my long-term girlfriend. Against this backdrop how could I possibly 'know' that I was going to walk away from it all and live in Australia? But it was there; a faint, but sure 'knowing' sensation.

  Over the coming weeks, I listened to this 'knowing'. I tried to come to terms with it and asked myself, 'why' a lot. My ego tried to rationalise it and make sense of it. Over time, the answers started to emerge. I didn't know it at the time but this deep 'knowing' was a subconscious, intuitive knowledge that the friend was my future wife. I went. The result of trusting this intuition is that ten years on I am happily married to my soulmate and we have two lovely children.

  Not everyone listens to these messages. People often try to keep them under wraps. I would not be unleashing some of the power of my true potential now if I hadn't listened then.

  More recently when running a corporate leadership programme, I felt as if something was waiting for me outside. It was such a clear feeling that it distracted me from the last hour of the day's programme. I kept glancing outside to see if anyone was there. The grounds of the country house hotel were stunning and it was a beautiful summer's evening. Knowing by now that I should listen to these intuitions, when the programme finished, I went outside to see what was waiting for me. As I walked around the grounds I could feel something welling up inside me.

I was drawn to an old stone bench where I sat down and enjoyed the garden. Suddenly I became aware that my future was not limited to programmes intended to develop corporate leadership and results. It was much broader. I was here to enable everyone to reach their true potential, not just businesspeople. The feeling was so deep and heartfelt that it moved me to tears. On the phone to my wife I told her, 'This isn't it' and began writing this book in earnest almost immediately.

The place that this message came from was a place of almost complete silence, of overpowering love and of unimaginable power. It was beautiful and profound. This was one of the strongest intuitions I ever had.

I just *knew*.

Coincidence

I was coaching an individual who was off work with depression. We were at his house as he was not back at work yet and he had two big dogs that were lying in the room. The session went quite deep as we explored his situation. He finally seemed to make some kind of breakthrough. He sighed and looked up at me.

'I can't do everything all the time,' he said quietly. The dogs suddenly went mad, barking their heads off. As he experienced a step change in awareness, I think they felt the significant change in what he was resonating in the zero point field. Nothing else changed at that exact moment to set them off. What he had just become aware of was hugely significant for him and his life. What he was resonating deep below his iceberg would have changed significantly at that moment. Dogs are good at listening to the zero point field and their sudden loud barking at those words sent a shiver down my spine.

Most coincidences are more subtle than this and may require some translation. My diving instructor always said to me, 'If you look out for the small things, you won't miss the big things.' Here are yesterday's examples of two small things just to give you an idea:

My wife asked me if there were any films to record in the evening. I replied that I had already set the DVD to record *Gladiator*.

'That's funny,' she replied, 'I was just downstairs thinking of that film.' It turned out that she had been thinking about it as I was setting the DVD recorder upstairs to record it. I think she had picked up on what I was doing through the zero point field and this triggered her thoughts of the specific film I was recording.

Ten minutes later I was helping my son clean his teeth. I noticed that his brush was well worn, so changed it. My wife then said, 'His toothbrush needs changing.'

I realised that in all the preceding years of brushing, I had never once looked at the brush head, let alone changed it. I must have picked up on my wife's thoughts in the zero point field. Something quietly 'nudged me' to act differently to the way I usually did. On this evening we were clearly well 'tuned in' to each other, even though we were not giving each other undivided attention. We were simply 'open' and we 'let come'.

By the way it isn't always like that in our house. I bet you have had similar experiences with loved ones though. Ever bought each other the same Christmas present? Ever gone to phone them just as they ring you? Have you any idea what the probability of those kind of things happening purely by chance is?

... or of course all the above examples could have been down to pure coincidence.

Coincidence fascinates me. It is often used in the modern world to imply 'complete luck' or 'an unconnected chance in a million'. Actually the origins of the word lie more in 'a perfect meeting of angles'. When something happens that is 'so perfect, it couldn't be luck', the implication is exactly that – it wasn't pure luck. Luck could not have created such a perfect meeting of angles. The implication is that there are other forces at work. The scientifically proven behaviour of quantum particles at last gives us a rational basis for how these things could happen.

If coincidences were rare and had little use, I wouldn't be so fascinated by them. In fact they become more common-place when you are on the road to unleashing your full potential; in fact far too common for this to be a coincidence. It is as if when you make the decision to live out your true potential and your ego and soul stop battling, the world meets you half way. Listening to and treating coincidences with respect has been highly rewarding when guiding me on my journey towards my true potential. I see no reason why it should not be the same for you.

I hope you know by now that I am a rational kind of person. I did maths A-level. I know about probability. We talked about life's dice earlier. You make rational choices that determine the number of sides on life's dice. It is only by tapping into some of the more radical areas of the One para-digm that you get to load your dice too.

Your ability to use the zero point field effectively, act on the messages it has for you and live in the One paradigm will enable you to load life's dice in your favour. Of course with everything it is a personal choice, but I always make a mental note of coin-cidences and reflect on what quantum communication could have produced them. I ask myself 'What's the message here?' For example the small personal examples I shared above happened last night. I took that as a sign to include them as examples as I sit here writing these words today. I trust that my higher potential is guiding me correctly. I trust that it was useful for you in some way.

Now we are getting into the nitty gritty of what this new paradigm has to offer. Now we are starting to get into the practical stuff. It may be that you were enjoying this book and now it is making you feel uneasy. That's fine.

Analogy/Meaning

When you are open and actively 'sensing' the world around you, you sometimes 'notice' things. A picture or an event catches your attention more than it perhaps should do. Pay attention as your two-million-bit processor is likely to have made a link. It may be trying to give you a message through an analogy or attaching a meaning to what seems on the surface to be a comparatively banal event.

If everything is related, there is often a deeper meaning or analogy that is useful for you.

I had been trying to write this book for years and I was making progress when we had our second child. Although she was a dream baby, my wife was not well and for the best part of a year we lurched from one illness or problem to the next. With her unable to return to work, I shouldered the responsibility of income as well as supporting the family. Needless to say there was little room for writing. For a year I did not tap a key.

I tapped into very little intuition in that year. It was a hard 'doing' year. I questioned whether this was appropriate or whether I should have pursued my life goal more fervently. I pondered the lack of intuitive guidance. Was I off track and therefore separated from the power of One? Or was I on track and therefore not in need of guidance? I suspected the second. What's the good of writing a book whose key corner-stones are relations, connections and nature if as a result you are not there for the relations you are naturally most connected to in their hour of need? The words would not match the actions.

In December of that year my wife had a transformational moment during an appointment with her cranial osteopath. It seemed as if overnight all her troubles disappeared. Three weeks later on a blustery night, we stayed for our wedding anniversary in a lovely old hotel and were joyous. We considered what the next year might hold. A third child? Moving to a bigger house? Living in the country? An international assignment? We looked forward to getting on with things again with great excitement.

In the middle of the night I was woken by a banging noise. It sounded like a swing door somewhere below in the hotel. It kept me awake for a while, then I ignored it and fell asleep. Later I was woken again. I listened more carefully. It was more like a knocking noise. I went to the loo and heard it tap clearly just outside the door. I looked through the spy hole, but could not see anything. I opened the door and stood naked in the hallway. One of the old windows was not secured and as it blew open and shut it made the knocking noise. I shut it and went back to bed.

I couldn't sleep. I had a strange feeling. I kept thinking, 'Something's here, I know it'. There was a subtle difference surrounding the experience. It was something I had not felt for a while. There was a meaning here. I knew it. It gradually emerged for me.

Opportunity knocks. The window knocks. A window of opportunity. I had started this book, but fallen 'asleep' for the last year. The window was knocking again. A brief window maybe. Intuitively it felt like a twelve-month window in which to hear the calling to complete this book. I would get up and respond to it. I would complete it in a year. All I could think was, 'Come on, let's go!'

It was a stormy night when we went to bed – why was the window not knocking then? What changed to make it knock and create this event? Who would have opened it at 3am? What was the likelihood that of all the hundreds of leaded windows in this place, the one that knocked was directly opposite our room? We had requested our favourite room when we checked in, but it was not available, so we were allocated this one instead. It felt as if we were meant to stay in this room. I had to be opposite that window to receive this message.

Coincidence, a different feeling and a sense of knowing all combined to result in a strong analogy that held great meaning for me. It doesn't matter if you wouldn't attach this meaning to it as it was my experience, not yours. You may have attributed a different meaning or none at all – it could have just been an annoying inconvenience to you. That would of course be fine. It is what makes sense and holds meaning to *you* and *your* life at the moment you are in that is important, not anyone else. After all it is *your* two-million-bit processor that is at work and no one else has the same two-million-bit processor or iceberg as you.

This event and the meaning it held for me had a significant effect. It brought me a sense of urgency that was lacking before. It focused me on the task at hand. The words flowed easily after that and the book was written within the year. The meaning I attributed to the coincidences of that night spurred me on and helped me to unleash more of the power of my true potential.

Visions

Whilst I was in the depths of depression I attempted to find another job. On the one hand I was short listed for a six-figure regional director's role in a multinational company and had the final interview approaching; on the other I could join my wife as an independent leadership consultant and coach. With a young baby, a mortgage, a part-time income and depression, the former seemed to be the one I ought to pursue. However something was nagging at me and I felt confused when I considered the pros and cons of each.

My coach suggested I go on a Vision Quest – a version of what the North American shamans do as a rite of passage. They go off into the wilderness, spend time in nature and gain clarity on what it is that they are here to do. I accepted the challenge and planned a trip to the Lake District in January. It would be wet, cold and lonely.

I found wandering over the hills alone to be incredibly therapeutic. I felt the 'tangled spaghetti' of my decision begin to naturally unravel and I gained a lot of clarity. I could at last feel the heavy fog of depression begin to lift. The second day was blissful. Whenever my soul said, 'stop here', I obeyed, unquestioning. I was in the moment. I felt completely 'open'.

As I sat on a bench over looking Derwent Water, I was suddenly aware of a being walking up and sitting on the other end of the bench. I was shocked and sat bolt upright. It was not really there, but the presence was palpable. I could actually see it faintly in the real world. My conscious ego brain took over and tried to comprehend what this was and it immediately began to fade. I silenced it, deciding just to 'be with it' and see what happened. The vision gained strength again and became clear.

He was a slim, well groomed man. He had slightly greying hair, was dressed smartly and had an air of success about him. He started talking. I couldn't make out the exact words, but his voice was deep and authoritative. I looked at my muddy boots compared to his shiny, black shoes and felt inadequate; inferior. The gist of what he was saying was that this was a serious matter; that I should grow up; that I had responsibilities. Taking the director's job that was within my grasp was sensible, the right choice and would lead to a successful corporate future.

I started to lose interest in his droning very quickly, but on he went. Suddenly it seemed to me that he represented a future self. Someone I could be in my life depending on the decisions I made in the next few days. In the same instant, I knew he was a future self I did not want to be. The moment I realised this, he lost his authority. I smiled. I knew I could be him if I wanted to, but I had chosen not to. I laughed out loud across the lake as he droned on.

Then my nose tingled and I felt tears welling in my eyes; partly because it was a moving experience and partly because I was sorry for this future self. I felt a sense of loss. Eventually I walked away, leaving him droning on and fading on the bench.

Depending on your set of beliefs, knowledge and wisdom, you will have a view as to what that was. I had never experienced anything like it before in my life. I'm sure some people would say it was an angel, others would say it was a ghost and others would say I had gone mad. Was the man *actually there*? I don't think so. I don't think anyone else could have seen him. I think it was the two-million-bit processor of my subconscious speaking to me in pictures. After two days of silence in the hills, I had quietened my ego enough for my soul to get a look in. I was in a calm, quiet, open frame of mind. I felt at peace. I 'let come' before I even knew about letting come.

It was a shock to me. I did not feel in control of it. It seemed to come from outside rather than me generating it. I had never felt this before, but then I had never spent two whole days alone in nature, effectively deepening a meditation over time.

The message needed translating and I translated it in a way that made sense to me. You might have translated it differently and that would have been fine – you are living your life and I am living mine.

It was as if that first shocking vision opened a door for me. A door to access intuitive visions more easily. As a result there were other visions that day. One was of a scrawny naked 'being' jumping around on the rocks of a stream. This spoke to me of lean times combined with a nimbleness. If I was going to become an independent leadership consultant and coach, I would need to go back to my hunter-gatherer roots to find work and build up a client base. No more steady, fat cat income for me. I would be judged and rewarded in line with my abilities. I liked that. It seemed more natural.

I had moments of absolute clarity alone in the hills. I gained a perspective that was greater than anything I had experienced before. The confusion had gone.

I had taken a significant step forward in uncovering my life purpose.

These two examples may sound spectacular to you and writing them down here, they do seem quite dramatic, but at the time the visions were very subtle and unassuming. If you wait to be slapped in the face by a multicoloured vision or a booming voice that gives you clear instructions, you will wait for a long time. That is the kind of intuition that the modern world paradigm would demand; neon lights! No wonder people rarely experience intuition if that is the only level of subtlety their radar is set to receive.

I find that often visions somehow become more concrete when I think back to them. At the time they are often a quiet and fleeting thought that could easily be missed. Rather than thinking, 'That's silly', I created the mental stillness and space for them to be and caught the faint suggestion of them. I 'held' the intuitive vision long enough to enable it to 'stick' with me. It was only afterwards that I considered the translation of what it meant to me.

This is another important thing to notice about intuition. It often comes and gets you rather than the other way round. It is relatively straightforward to separate out an ego-generated daydream from an intuitive 'vision'. The intuition creeps up on you. It is often resisted by your ego. It may make you feel uncomfortable. It comes from the soul and the ego would rather be in charge. Once you become more practised and welcome intuition as a part of your everyday life, the ego starts to accept the new status quo and intuition becomes easier to access. The ego stands to one side.

Nurturing and Translating

Do you think I have some special power that you don't have? I don't. I believe we are just the same. We have the same biological history. We are related. We are connected. Why would you not have the same ability? When you create a safe environment for people to share their intuitions (like the first-timer we spoke about earlier), you would be amazed what turns up.

- *On a scale of 1–10, how much do you listen to your own intuition?*

- *When was the last time you listened to your own or another's intuition when it contradicted what your ego wanted to hear?*

Think of a specific problem that has been rolling round and round for some time and doesn't seem to want to go away. If you asked the people involved to share their soul's intuition about what was the root of the problem, what do you think they would say?

- *Take a quiet moment to reflect. What does your soul's intuition say about the root of the problem?*
- *So what will you do next?*

I challenge you to ask people who are close to you and who trust you to share their intuitions. Make it safe for them. This will only work if you really, truly, authentically want to listen. Remember that they will smell it if it is inauthentic and that will hamper results. See what turns up, reflect on it and record the results in your notebook.

Keep your eye out for your own intuition. Practise accessing it. Make space for it. Exercise that muscle.

Combining the Transmitter and the Receiver

Tapping into the power of your two-million-bit processor through the medium of intuition is powerful enough, but things really start to kick off when you combine it with deep iceberg work. Developing deeper self-awareness enables you to access intuition more easily. As you become more aware of the inner voice of your ego, you are better placed to silence it. The more personal awareness and development work you do, the fewer self-limiting beliefs get in the way. The more you understand your deeper soul, the more you are able to listen to what it has to say.

The more aware you are of yourself and your own iceberg, the more able you are to appreciate other people's too. This development in awareness leaves people more open to suggestions and meaning from elsewhere. Intuition can offer direct feedback from the zero point field as to what you are resonating or dissonating at any point in time.

Are you on the right track? As I wrote these words I considered the question myself. 'Right now is what I'm writing on the right track?' I looked out of the window of the train I was on and saw tracks gleaming in the late afternoon sun. The meaning I attached to this was a clear affirmation: 'You are on the right tracks'. I smiled and continued. It seems as though the Oneness of the world is looking out for you. It can be playful as well as moving. It doesn't always have to be deep. It is there to help you.

Life Purpose

Only a few people believe they have a life purpose. Fewer people have asked themselves what it is and even fewer actually come to some kind of answer. The questions you have to ask yourself need deep consideration

* *What is life all about?*
* *Why am I here?*
* *What is the unique purpose that I was put on this earth to achieve?*

You can't answer these fundamental questions using only your seven-bit ego processor. Sure your senses can help, but life's ultimate questions are just too profound to answer relying on them alone. It would be like taking on the world's most complicated equation with an abacus. It would take longer than a lifetime to solve.

You need to understand your iceberg to deepen self-awareness. You need to identify your soul and your ego. You need to reduce your dependence on ego thinking and enable your soul to shine forth. Going through this process can make you feel vulnerable, but it enables you to resonate with more power at a higher frequency in the zero point field. As long as you are true to your soul, the Oneness of the zero point field meets you half way and you can utilise intuitive thinking to help you decipher the ultimate question of your life.

• *What are you here to do?*

One definition of self-actualisation is achieving purpose. How can you do this unless you know what your purpose is? By nature, it serves as an anchor to your soul. It helps check the ego when it gets carried away. It helps you to more instinctively feel when you are on the right track on your journey through life. When the winds of misfortune blow and the storms of the ego rage, it is always there; a tiny speck of light on the hillside, guiding you back home.

Being on the right path *is* the destination. You could be there today. If you can clearly see your direction, you stand a better chance of being truly deeply happy and fulfilled on a real and perpetually abundant level.

If you have no idea what you are here to do, that's fine. If you develop self-awareness and listen, you will start to gain direction. If you are open, the Oneness of the world will help you answer your questions. There is something about the way you deeply resonate when on the quest for meaning that invokes more of the earth's power.

• *Expect to be met half way.*
• *Expect some strange coincidences.*
• *Expect intuitions rich in signs and meaning.*

For what it is worth, I would currently define my life purpose as 'to enable people to be the best they can be'. No surprise that this book talks about unleashing the power of your true potential then. This book is a key part of my life purpose, but it is not the purpose itself. Publishing it will not *give* me fulfilment as you can never 'have' fulfilment. It is not the target, it is not the end. It is part of the journey. I have some ideas about what will happen afterwards, but a lot of what happens next will be down to you.

Your life purpose will play a part in the deeper meaning of all life. For example, 'Enabling people to be the best they can be' will enable the human race to evolve. That fits in with the meaning of life that was defined earlier. Your life purpose will fit in to that too and support the meaning of life at some level – it is the natural way of things and nature is the greatest power.

A life purpose may be bigger than you. You will have an important part to play, but it may not be achievable on your own or in your lifetime. However, if you identify and work towards your life purpose it can be deeply fulfilling and enable you to unleash the power of your true potential.

Although my life purpose seems clear to me now, I know that change is natural. As I evolve through my life, so too may my purpose. Beneath my purpose are more detailed goals that will enable me to live the purpose. This book is one of them.

As a result of the profound experiences on my vision quest I made my decision. I called the head-hunter and told him that I would not be attending the final interview. My wife and I planned our finances, tightened our belts and I set myself up as an independent leadership consultant and coach. The plan was to build up enough business between us to allow us to live securely and afford me the time to write this book.

I didn't know it then, but the day we reached that sustainable income level, the universe gave me a nudge in the garden of the country house where 'something was waiting outside'. It was as if the Oneness of the world said, 'You have enough clients and sustainable repeat business now. You are secure enough to start part two of your plan. Now get writing that book.'

- *Where is your special place in nature?*

Plan a few days alone there. Walk in the rain, sit under trees, do whatever comes naturally. Reconvene with nature. Feel the truth of your ancestors living off the land. Watch nature and learn from it rather than disregarding it.

- *Quietly take stock of your life. How did you expect it to turn out?*
- *How has it turned out so far?*
- *So what next?*

If you have any pressing problems, issues or decisions to make, quietly consider them as you walk. The ancient act of walking brings a natural rhythm to our considerations. Do not expect blinding lights. Don't look out for visions, for you are unlikely to access them consciously. Relax.

Spend some time forgetting everything. Empty your mind. Stop thinking.

Just be.

On your return, consider what you learnt and record your thoughts in your notebook. If your vision quest was valuable time, plan in another one in a few months' time. Consider the clarity you get from this kind of time in relation to identifying your life purpose.

The Next Level

Understanding the One paradigm sets up the fundamental cornerstones of the world we live in. Appreciating that everything is connected, everything is related and that nature is the greatest power enables us to view life from a different perspective.

Developing self-awareness of our own iceberg enables us to understand ourselves at a deep level. We are able to identify our ego and our soul, bringing the power of our two-million-bit processor to bear. We gain clarity about the choices we are making. We develop new 'choice points' as we make the ego step aside. We make more conscious choices about which of life's dice we want to roll each day. We resonate at a higher frequency in the zero point field and we therefore bring more of what we need at a deep level into our lives.

From this quieter place of being, with the ego stepping aside and aligning behind the soul, we have more presence. We are stiller. We are able to give people true undivided attention, without the ego butting in. We are able to just be and 'let come'. We are more open to the intuitive messages present in the zero point field where all particles communicate with each other. We begin to *load* our dice as we make use of knowledge outside the realm of normal perception. It is not magic. Animals do it. We get closer to the greatest power (nature) and we gain valuable information that guides us and gives us a competitive advantage when pursuing our life purpose.

There is a state of being that represents the ultimate level of resonance, but before we get into that, it is vital that you cement the insights this book has offered so far.

Take time out to practise.

Exercise your intuition 'muscle'. Keep a note of what happens in your notebook.

When you are confident and know these things to be true from your own personal experience, pick up the book and continue.

Fierce Love: The Ultimate Resonance

In the early days of writing this book, I mentioned the notion of Oneness amongst a group of friends. Immediately they were interested and asked me to elaborate.

'Oh great', I thought. 'I have this notion going through my head that has arisen out of the whole of my experience of life; I think I might want to write a book about it and suddenly I've got to explain it in front of a group of people.' At that point I was not even quite sure exactly what it was, let alone how to explain it clearly. It felt highly embarrassing.

'Well you know the evolutionary tree?' I began and then rattled through a rather self-conscious explanation of the ideas behind the first three chapters of this book. As the conversation deepened I found myself grappling with how to explain the fundamental essence of One.

I offered a couple of half-baked possibilities, but they didn't hit the mark. Then there was a silence as I racked my brain. I quietly became aware of something rising up within me. It was as if the trunk of my body was being filled with water. As it rose towards my throat I became aware that I was about to say something, but I had no idea what it was going to be. It was weird. Looking back on it now I realise that my soul had something to say. I looked up.

'Love,' I said and tears filled my eyes.

In my life to that moment, this was the closest I had got to understanding the true meaning of that word.

I am 6 foot 4. I was sitting there in a rugby shirt. I had spent a lot of my life in pubs indulging in pretty laddish behaviour. Suddenly this big man was discovering that his number one value was love.

I was a bit surprised by that.

I was even more surprised when I had a conversation with one of my best mates later that week. He was talking about what he considered to be most important in life and it sounded awfully like love to me.

'What do you think is the most important thing in life?' I asked him, suspiciously.

There was a pause.

'Love,' he said.

He is even bigger than me – a 6 foot 6 rugby player! I couldn't believe it. What was going on?

Fierce Love

The word Love is banded around liberally, but our understanding of what it really means has become tainted by the modern world. Naturally as most of us operate predominantly in the ego stage of development on Maslow's hierarchy, we tend to place an ego or identity around the word. We then end up with all sorts of different types of love that we can make sense of.

Puppy love, young love, shallow love, tough love, cupboard love, deep love, conditional love, forbidden love, obsessive love, unhealthy love, all-encompassing love, falling in love, falling out of love, love lost, love of your life, love of the game, in love with himself, you love it! The list is endless. These terms attempt to make sense of different aspects of life and whilst they may be useful in the modern world, they water down and distort the true meaning of the word 'love'. They create separate versions of love with a little 'l'.

Whilst not wanting to place another ego around love, an adjective that describes the true nature of Love is 'Fierce'. *Roget's Thesaurus* has 'robust', 'intense', 'powerful', 'passionate', 'eager' and 'unbridled' as synonyms for fierce and these appropriately capture just some of the aspects of this most fundamental power of Love.

Love with a capital 'L' is central to most religions. Almost every song that has ever been in the charts sings about it. Almost every film touches on it. This definition of Fierce Love is not bound by stereotypes and expectations. It is not limited to the watered-down versions of love that we encounter in the modern world. It is not limited to the love that we feel for our husband, wife or children. It is unbridled, unconditional and free. It is an internal way of being. It also resonates perfectly with the One perspective. It is incredibly powerful. In fact it is transformational.

The Ultimate Resonance from Within

When talking about oneness with my friends that day, my soul taught me a fundamental lesson. It was the realisation that love underpins everything. Love *is* the One perspective in its purest form.

If you could live life immersed totally in the inescapable truths that everything is related, everything is connected and nature is the greatest power, then the ultimate manifestation of that would be Love.

Love is the gateway to the One perspective.

The One perspective helps us to understand how the world works 'out there'. It helps to guide our actions, but if we are 'trying' to do the 'right' thing all the time, living in the One perspective can feel hard. If we are not careful we will end up beating ourselves up and 'trying hard'. That doesn't sound very natural to me and nature is the greatest power. There is a danger that we will end up constantly questioning what we 'should' be doing and make life heavy and rule-laden.

But Love is the underpinning force of the One perspective. It is the lynchpin that links the inner and outer worlds. It is generated from within and you are in charge of that. You decide consciously or unconsciously what you Love and how much Love you choose to show. You decide how much Love you allow to flow through you in the zero point field. You get to choose whether to make it a struggle or whether to make it easy. It has to start with you.

If you want to change the world from the inside out, then this is the inside bit.

All the things that are out of balance in the modern world come from a lack of understanding of the outside world and a lack of Love emanating from the inside world of the individual. This creates a heartless cycle bent on building egos, separateness and scarcity. Love by its very nature creates understanding. Where we do not understand, Love generates curiosity rather than judgement. Love says a resounding, 'Yes!' to life and all that it brings.

If you assume the best in others, the law of attraction will load life's dice for you, making it more probable that people will rise to their full potential in their interactions with you. If you assume the worst, the way you interact with them will tend to encourage a result in line with your low expectations. I have seen it happen time and time again.

Love also tends to be contagious. Infectious viruses are a natural and successful phenomenon – they have been around for millions of years. Love is like a positive disease; the more you put it out there, the more other people catch it. The light of Love flickers a little brighter within them and they pass a little of that light on to others.

The light of the ultimate power of Love is not limited. It is not like a battery that eventually runs out. It is free. After all it is the power of the zero point field. It is the unfettered resonance of our soul. It is our highest state of being. It makes us feel happy, fulfilled and warm. All we have to do is open up and let it flow through us into our actions and behaviours. We act like a channel for an inexhaustible, abundant, power of incredible magnitude. When Love powers our actions we become significantly more powerful and influential.

Think of a time when you have received this kind of unconditional Love from a stranger, whether it be helping you out when you were in dire need or simply holding the door open for you and smiling. What difference did it make to you?

When people extend that kind of Love to me, I notice and I smile. It gives me a lighter spring in my step. It helps me to see that the world is actually full of lovely people (like you). I reflect on how 'Oneful' their actions are. I am inspired to do the same for someone else even if it is just in a small way. People respond to it in kind, perpetuating its virus-like domino effect.

The Angry Neighbour

Where we used to live, one of our neighbours had a low wall. One day my young son and a friend sat on it and chatted. They were just like two old men, chewing the fat as they discussed the things that young children find important.

I came out of the house later to find the neighbour standing before them. I will never know exactly what had been said, but the zero point field was crackling with the anger that had just been unleashed. I could feel it as a burning sensation in my arms. As the neighbour walked away, the boys scrambled in desperation to get off the wall. My son's friend burst into tears and ran in fear back to his house.

I knew a little about the neighbour and was therefore aware that his iceberg contained some difficult experiences by anyone's standards. He saw the situation through his ego's glasses. His ego believes that everyone is out to get him, so that is what he sees everywhere. That is how his life therefore turns out for him; creating a self-fulfilling prophecy that generates demons and problems where others see none. His brittle ego then has to fight in the negative world that he has created to retain some semblance of power over others. Even if it means that little children have to cry.

My son walked into the sitting room and sat on the sofa, looking as white as a sheet. His eyes were wide in fear. He was quiet.

'Are you OK?' I asked.

His face slowly crumpled and he burst into tears, sobbing into his hands.

I don't think either boy in their life to date had ever experienced such anger. I was immediately reminded of similar experiences in my childhood. I remember the deep hurt I used to feel in my stomach, the physical reaction, the fear whenever I saw the person again. I remember the deep emotional wound that my soul received.

As I looked at my son, so vulnerable and upset, my conflict-avoiding ego first wanted to say, 'Leave it. He should not have been sitting on the wall. The neighbour was right.'

From a place of Fierce Love, my soul quietly, but firmly said, 'No'.

My ego quickly jumped in again and said, 'You're right. How dare he do that to your son! Go straight round there and give that neighbour a taste of his own medicine! Tear strips off him! You are a big man; you can scare him just as much as he can scare a little boy! This might even warrant something physical! Let's go!'

From a place of Fierce Love, my soul quietly, but firmly said, 'No'.

It was strange, but I suddenly felt as if I had been transferred into a real life role-play where the exercise brief and the people were real. I could even sense hidden observers making notes. It seemed as if the zero point field was saying, 'He's writing a book about Love, so let's see how he deals with this!'

I took a deep breath and picked up my son, giving him a big hug.

'It's OK,' I told him gently as I started walking over to the neighbour's house.

'Where are we going?' he sobbed.

'To talk to him.'

'No!' he wailed, but my soul knew it was the right thing to do. This event would have a negative place in my son's iceberg if we didn't do something about it right now. As I walked, I had no idea what I was going to say or do. I had not prepared any clever speech. I just went round there with a firm belief that if I approached the situation from a place of Fierce Love of myself and others (both my son and the neighbour) that it had the potential to be transformational.

His iceberg meant that the explosion which left two small boys crying was the best he could do. He actually needed some Fierce Love, not to be judged, not to be let off the hook, not to be abused back.

I rang the door bell. The neighbour answered and he was immediately angry and highly defensive. We talked. I came at the interaction through a perspective of pure calm and Love. My 'being' of Fierce Love seemed to produce an aura around us. I felt supremely confident in myself, the neighbour and my son. I felt that if I stood in this difficult place, resonating and talking from a place of deep Unconditional Fierce Love, something amazing would happen.

My exact words were unimportant; it was all about how I was *being*. I gave the neighbour my undivided attention. I listened with his ears. I didn't force my opinion on him. I developed empathy. I soaked up how it was to be him. I understood his point of view. As I did, his anger began to subside. With nothing to resist or fight against, it began to lose its grip over him.

Then, without making him wrong or me right, I shared my perspective on the event. I did this from a place of Fierce Love, which helped the words land gently rather than aggressively. Having listened to the neighbour and shown him respect and Fierce Love, I expected the same in return. The law of attraction was operating and against the odds it was returned. By the end of the exchange, I think we understood each other a little better. Fierce Love made this exchange one of understanding rather than aggression.

I suggested my son give the neighbour a hug and apologise for sitting on the wall. My son had a physical aversion. As I gently pushed him forward, he struggled to get away from this 'demon' in a state of panic. The neighbour saw this and suddenly the tough, aggressive exterior of his ego completely collapsed before my eyes. The look on his face changed as his soul became aware of what his ego had done to a small child. His soul suddenly shone through.

The neighbour rushed off into the kitchen and returned with a chocolate bar. He knelt down to my son's level, offered the peace token, apologised and gave him a big hug. My son smiled, also apologised and hugged him back.

I think we all walked away from that doorstep interaction slightly dazed and confused about what had happened. I can't tell you how unlikely that result was given the ingredients of the situation. It would have been a very long shot on life's dice. But we did it. All of us together made something incredible happen. From a place of Fierce Love, life's dice were well and truly loaded in Love's favour.

The two-million-bit resonance of Fierce Love always trumps the seven-bit ego. Always.

Following this, my son said hello to the neighbour when they met in the street. They even wished each other happy birthday.

Somehow this initially aggressive conflagration was transformed by Fierce Love into a deepening of our relationship together. It was not smoothed over. It was not escalated. It was transformed.

This is a small personal example of how Fierce Love can significantly change the way we choose to make the world work. It was just a drop in the ocean.

The way the world works right now is made up of drops just like this. We all have the potential to create this every day of our lives. We have a choice.

The neighbour had a choice as to how to approach the situation. Maybe next time, he will come at it from a slightly more loving place. If he does, he will begin to ascend towards that self-actualisation apex rather than being stuck in the ego trap. A bit of Fierce Love will have rubbed off on him, so he stands a better chance. He certainly stands a better chance than if I had attacked him back, fuelling his belief that people are out to get him.

- *What issue do you see in your life that you could use
  Love to transform? This could be an unresolved dispute
  or an ongoing misunderstanding between you and
  another.*
- *Accept that the people involved (including you) are
  doing the best they can at this moment in time given
  their icebergs. For a moment imagine that you are
  them. As you look at the situation from their
  perspective, what understanding does it give you?*
- *Now consider what would happen if you viewed the
  situation and the people from a place of Fierce Love
  without any judgement. What would change?*

Try it and see if it works. Don't worry about who comes out on
top or who is right and who is wrong – that's the ego talking.
You may have to take a bigger step towards them and put aside
your ego-powered pride. This may not feel 'fair' to your ego. If
so, just notice that and put it to one side. It is OK to give away
more than your 'fair' share because the Love we are talking
about is not finite. Just channel the abundant power of Unconditional Love at the issue and see what happens to you and
them.

- *Having had a go at Fierce Love, consider what would
  happen if you lived your whole life from that place.*
- *If you engaged with all people consistently from this
  place, how would life change for you?*

When an interaction occurs that would normally trigger an
instant emotional response in you (like someone bumping
into you with their shopping trolley or pushing in front of
you), press the 'pause button'. Rather than venting your
emotion or suppressing it, take the perspective of Fierce
Love. Let the event wash over you. Accept it. Assume the best
in the other person rather than the worst. We all make
mistakes.

I challenge you to live one day in a place of Fierce Love;

every interaction, every person, every moment; Fierce Love for all. Capture how the day was for you. Then decide if you want to do it again tomorrow.

Love is the ultimate. It is free. It is abundant. It powers the Oneness of the world. 'All' you have to do is open up to its presence and then let it flow through you. The question is, will you give Fierce Love a chance, and when?

The Worldwide Impact

Unfortunately the modern world does not encourage Fierce Love. Notice how the current norm of individual egoic responses is played out on a global level too. Terrorist acts by a few individuals have been repaid with military action against whole countries. The 'other side' has been depicted by many as 'evil' (on both sides). Rather than Fierce Love of the whole, people have taken the modern world view of separateness and demonised each other.

The result of holding this perspective is many innocent deaths on both sides, heartache for mothers, fathers and children who have lost loved ones and even more reason for both sides to hate each other. It perpetuates the situation and makes things worse. We set up a dangerous cycle, but the ego loves it. It provides lots of roles and definitions to separate things. It allows egos to judge others' actions as being 'wrong', therefore making it right. This builds a brittle, fragile, surface-level sense of confidence. The modern world paradigm of separateness prevails.

It is a shame (but not a surprise given the modern world paradigm) that most people in charge of these kinds of decisions are highly identified with their ego. In the modern world, egos are celebrated. Successful politicians therefore tend to appeal to the ego-focused masses.

An approach of Fierce Love seeks to understand and consider the whole. It demonstrates true empathy to understand how something like acts of terrorism can occur. Fierce

Love understands that people only attack or lash out when they feel fearful or under threat (remember the saying, 'Attack is the best form of defence'?).

Fierce Love takes a balanced view of both sides, seeing the truth in both. It immediately accepts and forgives the past and focuses instead on the present and the future. It has high expectations of both sides. It Fiercely Loves both. From this assertive place transformational change is more likely. From this perspective age-old disputes and repeated cycles of disagreement, violence and death are more likely to be resolved.

Take any long-standing international dispute that is currently causing bloodshed. If both sides had met ten years ago and tabled an option of future actions that included both sides killing a significant number of their own innocent men, women and children over a decade with no resolution to the dispute, it would have been laughed at. But commonly this is the option that the egos involved actually agree, consciously or otherwise. Not only that, they could just as easily be about to sign up to the same plan for the next ten years if nothing changes.

The power of Fierce Love can resolve significant long-standing problems if we give it a chance. It can grant us access to that uplifting, fulfilling life at the apex of Maslow's hierarchy right now.

Do you remember the wonderful 'future world' described at the start of the book? That's what results when the virus of Fierce Love spreads out across the population. That's what happens when we create an epidemic. That's what happens when people start to see a different way and say, 'I'm going to have a go at that too'. That's what happens when a significant number of people break free from the ego trap and evolve behaviourally into the self-actualisation level that they are ready for.

As Albert Einstein said, 'Problems cannot be solved by the same level of thinking that created them.'

We have to ask ourselves, 'If it really is that easy, if it really makes such a huge difference to people's lives including my own, why are we not all living life from a place of Fierce Love?' Why are we here, when we could be there? The answer is that there are two key barriers that the modern world puts in our way: scarcity and judgement.

Scarcity

The modern world paradigm prefers us to focus on scarcity and fear rather than abundance and confidence. In a scarce world where love is defined as something you 'give' away to others, you'd better ensure you are going to get something back. If you have a finite reserve of love to give away, you'd better not give freely of anything or you could run out.

The ego keeps score. How nice was I to that person? What did I give away? What did they give me back? Is that fair? If not I'll withdraw my love because I am pouring a scarce resource down the drain. How egotistical to imagine that we 'own' a reserve of Love. Love is not ours to own, it is ours to channel. It is ours to 'be' for free, whenever we want.

Scarcity is driven by the ego. The ego wants more of everything and when it can't get enough it says, 'Look! Scarcity!' On the other hand the soul doesn't need anything. It just is. It takes a more balanced and holistic view of the world.

What happens when you leave a vacant lot empty? Weeds start to grow through the cracks in the concrete for free. After a while, a bush takes root for free. Animals appear, make the most of the surroundings, set up home and have offspring for free. Eventually trees take root and over time you have a thriving ecosystem ... for free. Talk about abundance! All that stuff just happens for free! Abundance is the way of the world.

There is abundant power in the world; it's just that the ego gets in the way, placing value on money in the here and now over renewable, sustainable, cheap energy in the future. There is abundant food in the world; it's just that the ego would rather have more of it and make money from it than feed people in far-off lands.

There isn't enough Love out there because the ego in people focuses on separateness, fear and scarcity. It stops the natural virus of Love spreading. It keeps count. And of course this belief creates a self-fulfilling prophecy on a macro scale. Here's an example. Let's assume that a government believes in scarcity and separateness on a worldwide scale. This makes it feel separate from, mistrusting of, threatened by and competitive towards other countries. It is not going to act in a particularly Oneful way towards others. It is not going to be particularly holistic in its approach to global warming. Its policies are going to be to look after itself and largely ignore everyone else. The government ego is going to be distrustful of other countries because it sees them as separate, different and competing for scarce resources.

As global warming continues, one of the key effects of this kind of non-policy will be sea level rises. Low-lying countries are going to be faced with a new scarce resource (land!) and the ego will say, 'See I told you so!' Millions of people will become refugees. Homeless, starving people will flood into neighbouring countries acting as a huge drain on their natural reserves. The ego of their government will triumphantly say, 'See I told you so!'

Sometimes your actions from a Fiercely Loving perspective will not be returned. That is fine. You are not giving anything away, you are just 'being' in a way that makes your life personally fulfilling and rewarding. However your actions will often prompt those on the receiving end to reciprocate from a more Fiercely Loving place themselves. Then your experience of the world tends to be filled with more abundant expressions of Fierce Love rather than the pain and anguish that the modern world media would prefer we see.

Before Barack Obama was president, the US proposed an interceptor missile system that angered the Russians. They announced in return that they were going to deploy missiles and point them at NATO allies, which in turn angered the US.

The national egos seemed to be drawing each other into a new Cold War – lots of separateness and 'enemies' – the egos were rubbing their hands with glee.

When Obama became president, he announced that he would not be rushing through these plans to deploy US missiles. What happened? Did the Russians rub their hands with glee at the weak president and plan to bomb NATO allies as soon as possible? Of course not. They halted their plans to deploy missiles.

Like beliefs, taking a Fiercely Loving perspective creates a self-fulfilling prophecy that fosters the emergence and proliferation of the One paradigm and Love itself.

Judgement

Everyone is born with the innate ability to channel the power of Love into the world. Our soul resonates to its song, but often our upbringing stifles it. The Love that we do feel inside us often doesn't get out. A child that receives conditional love (for example, words or actions that seem consistent with the message, 'I'll love you as long as you're good') is given a strong message by its parents.

The 'stiff upper lip approach' that is prevalent in many Western societies stifles expressions of Love, especially in men. It stops it getting out. The culture we live in influences us to think that Love is not manly. It's not cool. It's much cooler (and easier) to be hard and aggressive. It is more macho. It fits the ego better and fits in with the modern world way where in a separate world of scarcity, you'd better defend yourself by fighting others. You are better off being selfish and looking after number one.

The ego is judgemental. It is constantly comparing and contrasting others. It tends to see the worst in others. It thinks up plenty of excuses for its own behaviour, making itself right, but then offers none of that generosity to others, because generosity is scarce too. Generosity comes in many different guises, from helping someone across the road, to spending time with someone and offering your services and help. It does not always have to be about money. A Oneful approach of 'helping the world go round' is a generous state of being.

An old man in my extended family broke down and wept on his wife's deathbed. As the tears rolled down his cheeks in an uncharacteristic show of Love, affection and emotion he said, 'I never told her that I loved her.'

They had been married for over fifty years. It would have meant the world to her to have heard that, but it took the shock of losing her for his ego to step aside and let his soul shine forth. Such is the cultural upbringing of many men. Openly express love? But what will others think? They'll think I've gone soft!

But what you can achieve from a place of Fierce Love is much more powerful on a deep level. Two examples of men who came at the world from a place of Fierce Love are Martin Luther King Jnr and Ghandi. There was nothing soft about them. They did not go around insincerely gushing to every-one that they loved them. That would have been love with a little 'l'.

They lived by a strong moral code that resonated with their soul. No matter what was thrown at them, no matter how bad things got, they controlled their ego and maintained an approach of Fierce Love for everyone – their opposition, their followers and everyone in between. They demonstrated clear self-actualisation behaviours on the world stage during troubled times. Many ego-level people in the world were not ready for the power of Love that emanated through them and their actions.

Times have moved on. The world is more ready now for true, deep expressions of Fierce Love than it has ever been.

You can't 'do' Love. There is no step by step guide. It is a state of being. However, there are some useful perspectives to 'be' in that will help you to develop your ability to invoke the ultimate power of your true potential. 'Awareness' and

'Acceptance' are two perspectives that are like train stations on the journey to allowing a free-flow of Fierce Love.

Awareness

One state of being that begins to invoke Fierce Love is that of awareness. Awareness of our iceberg, of our soul, our ego and the zero point field. Awareness of the way things and people are. This book's primary purpose is to spread this awareness; if you have read this far, answered the questions posed along the way and done the exercises, then you will have undoubtedly increased yours.

Many people go through most of their life in a dream-like, 'doing' state. They get caught up in the small unimportant details of their lives and for most of the time are unaware of the bigger picture. One of my greatest fears is waking up one day aged 50 and thinking, 'How on earth did I get here?' I regularly coach people in this kind of situation who say things like, 'I never dreamed of being an accountant, but here I am in a senior position in a global bank ... how did that happen?'

Going about life in a state of awareness means that you are constantly aware of your own iceberg and the lens that you see the world through. As a direct result of this you are also aware that everyone you encounter has their equivalent and they will be more or less aware of it than you. You do not know the details of their icebergs, but key drivers like the beliefs, motivators and values that cause their behaviour may become clearer to you as you listen at level 3.

Be aware of your position in the worldwide community. Maintain that awareness when you make purchasing decisions. Be aware of your position in the web of all life on the planet. Maintain that awareness when making decisions too. Sometimes ethical purchases can be confusing these days. If you want to make an ethical purchase, do not worry too much about whether to go ecologically sustainable, free trade or organic. Trust your intuition, do *something* from a perspective of Love and enjoy yourself. If everyone just did *something*, things would change extremely quickly. If you choose not to make an ethical decision, of course that too is fine. Either way the choices you make are conscious, not unconscious, and they are not laden with judgement.

Practise being aware. Take a week and see how aware you can be of everything, every minute of the day. Clearly you cannot 'do' awareness of everything all the time; you have to 'be' in that space.

- *How easy/hard is it?*
- *What takes you away from that state of awareness or consciousness?*
- *What will you do to help you stay present?*

Acceptance

Following on from awareness is acceptance. When you live consistently in awareness that everything is related, everything is connected and nature is the greatest power, you see the world around you operating differently. With the ultimate perspective on the biological, genetic and psychological history of our species and life on earth, a gradual awakening occurs.

This is the awakening of acceptance.

Everyone is on the same journey. Everyone is at different stages of that journey. Everyone has a unique iceberg, but everyone has an iceberg made up of beliefs, motivators, values, past experiences, etc. Everyone has hopes. Everyone has fears. Everyone is doing the best they can given their iceberg and their position on life's journey. The world is the way it is. We are the way we are. We begin to understand some of life's fundamental truths.

There is no point resisting what 'is'. It would be a pointless waste of effort. However the ego in us enjoys resisting things as it helps to define itself; 'I resist x', 'I can't stand y'. It all helps to define, divide and separate. This clearly resonates with the modern world paradigm as it is ego-dominated.

To resist any part of life is to resist a part of what makes up the whole and then you would resist a part of the ultimate Oneness of all things. One reason that Fierce Love is so elusive for many people (even some who are highly aware) is that they find acceptance difficult.

Acceptance begins at home.

The first person you need to accept fundamentally and wholeheartedly is you.

There is no point in wishing that a certain event hadn't happened in your past life story. It happened – that is a fact. If we don't accept it at a deep level, we harbour resentment and focus negative energy towards it. The energy of 'resistance' grants the 'undesirable' thing in your past life story more power than if you accepted it at a deep level. There is a danger that a past event can ruin the rest of your life.

You are great at some things – there are things you love to do; understand and accept that. You aren't so good at other things – there are some things you dislike doing; understand and accept that too. From a place of acceptance decide what you want to do about both.

Why would you want to resist something about you instead of accepting it?

A common misconception is that if everyone accepted everything on a deep level, then nothing would happen. Everyone would just sit around 'accepting' everything; life would be extremely boring. In fact deeply accepting all that is, helps you to move the focus and resonance of your thoughts away from resisting the past (where it cannot change anything and can only bring you down) and move it instead to the present and future where it can make a real, pragmatic difference.

When you can wholeheartedly accept yourself, you cannot help but wholeheartedly accept others. You say an almighty

'Yes!' to everything about the world. You remove blockages and resistance that short-circuit the flow of life's energy through your actions. You open up. The power of the zero point field flows freely through you, giving gravitas and influence to everything you do.

All ancient energy-based medicines like Chinese acupuncture, reflexology, massage and shamanism focus on the fact that physical blockages in your body are caused by psychological blockages in your life. The longer the blockage is present and the greater the intensity, the more likely you are to experience disease (dis-ease).

Your tolerance of others enables you to pause before engaging in automatic judgement, defence of your position or attack. Instead you can accept their position. They are part of this wonderfully interconnected web of life. You listen through pure unfiltered ears. You hear their story, you understand their perspective, you develop empathy. In this way, through acceptance you develop your awareness more and it sets up a self-fulfilling virtuous cycle that adds to your wisdom, understanding and power.

Just because you accept someone else's position does not necessarily mean you agree with it. You don't have to like/love everyone suddenly – that would be inauthentic. It is not about being puritanical. It is about taking a Fiercely Loving perspective when choosing who you want to have relationships with and who you want to let go of. You don't have to make other people wrong and you right. You can both be right, just different.

For example if someone is sapping your energy, you don't have to make them wrong. They may be unaware of what they do or they may be aware, but do not feel capable of anything different because of their iceberg. You get to choose from a Fiercely Loving place (of yourself and others) how much time you spend with that person. The Law of Non-Engagement states that if you do not engage with them, then they cannot take anything from you. If you do not play the game, then no one wins and no one loses.

You could choose not to spend time with them. You could choose to still spend time with them, but take a perspective that channels the abundant power of Love rather than one that makes you feel as if you are giving away your natural reserves. You could spend less time with them so that the balance between looking after your self and them works better. Whatever you decide to do, if you take a Fiercely Loving perspective, your behaviour will be in line with the One paradigm. Your actions will carry the gravitas and power of that ultimate perspective.

If it is raining you can focus your energy on complaining bitterly about the miserable weather to all who will listen. Alternatively you can marvel at how thanks to the naturally occurring hydrological cycle, water (the bringer of all life) just falls from the sky for free! The acceptance of that enables you to focus your energy instead towards making a differ-ence. You don't have to dance naked in the rain shouting about how wonderful it is to everyone you meet, you simply accept it and focus your energy where it is more useful for you that day.

If someone is rude to you, you could focus your energy on bitterly resenting them all day, telling everyone how awful people are these days. Alternatively you could accept that they were doing the best they could given their iceberg and focus your energy more productively on something else. No negative energy. No blockage.

I accept the way the world is poised right now, but that does not mean I just sit back and do nothing. I continue to work towards completing this book. I think it will make a difference to the future direction we choose to take. The level of influence it has will be a combination of my actions, your actions and the resonance of them in the zero point field. I accept that. I accept that some people will want to change and will get a lot from this book. I accept that others do not want to change and will find the concepts in this book threatening. Other people will think the whole thing is rubbish. That is all fine. That is all part of the journey.

Practise consistently maintaining a perspective of acceptance and tolerance. Replace judgement with curiosity. Seek to understand.

- *What happens from here?*
- *How do you find it?*
- *What things tend to suck you back into non-acceptance?*
- *These things that you can't stand probably say more about you than them. What is it that you can't be with?*
- *What will you do to maintain a perspective of acceptance when these kind of things next crop up?*

When you accept wholeheartedly what is, you advance up Maslow's hierarchy of needs.

You touch the apex.

Love

Awareness breeds acceptance. Acceptance breeds Love. Love of the whole. That includes Love of me, Love of you, Love of everyone else and a deeply accepting Love of everything that is.

Here lies another surprise for many people; the first person to Love is you. As you approach the world from a place of Love for all, you are included in that 'all'. You have just as much right to be Loved and accepted as everyone else in the world. No more and no less.

To Fiercely Love everyone does not mean that you just go around letting other people walk all over you and do what they want because you love them. That would be martyrful and you would become the victim. A victim mentality is an ego-based approach where you hold yourself in lower esteem than others. That can only result in love with a little 'l', which would not be a Real and Oneful view of the world. Remember it is about balance.

Through the eyes of Fierce Love your soul is able to see

the situation from a third person perspective. To see the whole. Self-awareness generates this in you. As part of that you see the same in others. You start to see the real picture. You accept that. You can then act from a place of Fierce Love. Sometimes you will step down and acquiesce. Sometimes you will step up and assert your position. Sometimes you will find a different, better way. From a Loving perspective you will be able to listen to your intuition more clearly and will be able to more accurately assess what the situation needs most.

From a place of Fierce Love you understand the values, motivators and beliefs of your iceberg and honour them. You navigate clearly using your inner compass. It gives you stability and direction when seas are rough. It gives power to your leadership. But this power does not trample on others because Fierce Love holds them in just as high regard as you. If it didn't then the ego would be talking again.

- *Fiercely Love and honour yourself for a day. Listen to what you want and honour that. What changes?*
- *Is it easy or hard to do? Why is that?*
- *What egoic influences are at work? These are the 'old stories' of thoughts and beliefs that limit your ability to Fiercely Love and respect yourself as much as other people.*
- *What 'roles' do you play out that interfere with a Fierce Love of yourself?*
- *What can you do about that?*

The Gift of Self-confidence

If you Fiercely Love yourself first, then you know that everything is OK; all that has been in your life, all that is yet to come. Just as developing more self-awareness enables you to develop empathy with others, developing Fierce Love for yourself enables you to truly, unconditionally, Fiercely Love others.

The Love that you hold for yourself will set the limit for the Love you can show others. If the only love you can show yourself is conditional and egoic, then that is the love that will channel through you. When you hold the highest regard, absolute respect and Fierce Love of yourself, that is when the power of Love flows through you into all that you do.

This perspective bestows upon you the gift of true self-confidence. You are able to be non-judgemental of yourself and others. There is no blame. There is no beating up of oneself. All that wasted energy resisting what is just melts away and in its place is left the quiet, powerful self-confidence of Love. If you try something and make a mistake it is no problem. There is no judgement. You learn from it and move on. You invoke evolution – the most powerful force in the world.

Our energy is channelled away from negative spirals and is focused instead towards what we really care about, what we are really here to do. Fierce Love sets us and everyone else free to be the best we can be. We stop holding others and ourselves small in order to make our egos feel better. We rise up with enormous self-confidence, courage and humility as we set foot in a world of self-actualisation and fulfilment of our true potential.

We walk along our chosen path in life steadily, deliberately and with conviction. We listen to others, we listen to our intu-ition and we act accordingly. We savour the journey; we admire the view along the way, as missing that would be to miss the point; the view from where we are right now is all that we actually ever have. We look back and see where we have come from, we look up at the road ahead and enjoy the subtle push and pull of both, but we are only ever in one place; the here and now.

The here and now. Right here right now. This very second. The second in your life when you read this word right here on this page. This moment is yours. This day is yours. You will only ever have it once in your life. What will you make of it?

From a place of Fierce Love, gravitas and self-confidence, it is time to take the next step down your life's road; a road and a direction that is of your choosing. Fierce Love is the place from which everything else is possible. When you approach the world from a place of Fierce Love, you generate it in others. You start to see it everywhere.

Ghandi said, 'I can't change the world, but I can change the world in me. You must be the change you want to see in the world.' When you channel Fierce Love, this comes true. Suddenly you see it. Everything is just as it is meant to be right now. We are all poised in this moment, ready for the next step. It is perfect. You end up seeing glimpses of a world very like the picture we painted at the start. You realise that it is coming, naturally. The more you act out of Fierce Love the more you help others to see that there is an alternative and they can choose to do the same. The more momentum builds, the more we bring that future place within our reach.

Fierce Love Invokes your True Potential

I know someone who enjoys writing. He attended creative writing classes and wrote a novel, enjoying the act of writing immensely. He is not a great completer-finisher at the best of times, but more than that, when the novel was completed, he put it on a shelf and never shared it with anyone.

The same writer completed a series of children's books for his son and illustrated them with pictures. His son loved them. Friends came round and when they read these stories at bedtime, they loved them too. 'You should do something with these,' they said. The writer smiled, 'Yes you are right,' he said and cheerfully placed them back on the shelf.

This writer admits that his past life story has left him with baggage that affects his self-confidence and stands between him and his true potential. He has realised that he holds a self-limiting belief that he is not an author. He believes that experience is essential. It seems that unless he can publish his work, he can not see himself as a writer. But his ego is ensuring that his work never has the chance to see the light of day. It is like when you go for your first job and everyone seems to want 'experience'. Like the chicken and the egg, you ask yourself, 'How can I get a job if I haven't got experience. How can I get experience if I can't get a job?'

Another problem for his ego is that when he writes, he writes from his soul. This is a vulnerable part of him that has not yet been laid bare before people, especially strangers. He has a sensitive soul at heart. His ego is stopping him from baring his soul to people for fear that this vulnerable aspect of his psyche will be ridiculed and attacked. As we have discussed, acting from fear disempowers you. It does not unleash the power of your True Potential.

If his ego is successful, he will be saved from potential ridicule. However he will also be saved from unleashing the power of his True Potential.

He is therefore stuck.

This writer is currently in the process of writing another book. Unless he overcomes the constant disturbance from his ego, one way or another, that work too will not see the light of day. This is a shame because I am lucky enough to have read his work and I believe many people will not only love what he has to offer, but they will truly benefit from it in real life. I hope he does it, not just for the good of himself, but for the good of the people who will bump into his work on their life journey. What he is writing about really does have the power to change the world.

As I write this, I do not know if this man has overcome the voice of his ego yet. He is aware of it. He accepts it. He strives to act from a perspective of Fierce Love. If he truly succeeds at this then he will be successful. Fierce Love of himself, other people and the wider world would not allow anything less.

If you are reading these words, you will know that he has been successful, because that writer is me.

The Call

I believe that you are amazing. I believe that you are unique. Already if you have completed the exercises in this book, you have been on an incredible journey that few people are brave enough to take on. I believe that you have incredible potential and if you Fiercely Love yourself, you will know that to be true.

I am special and you are special. Just because I have written this book does not mean that I am in a different category to you, I just chose to live and breathe my work as a leadership coach; the work I love. I just held myself accountable the way I would hold someone else accountable. I just developed some awareness around how my ego was holding me back. I then just chose to face some fears, take a risk and have a go at being the best I could be instead of hiding my light under a bushel.

- *How do you get in the way of your own success (i.e. limit what your soul knows you are capable of)?*
- *When does your ego tend to hold you back (with self-limiting beliefs or unhelpful perspectives)?*
- *With awareness of this comes 90% of the solution, so what will you do differently next time this happens?*

If you hear your ego trying to trip you up, you don't have to beat yourself up about it. Just notice it, thank it for its advice and tell it that this time you are not going to take it.

Fierce Love propels you into the self-actualisation apex of Maslow's hierarchy. In this state, at a deep soul level you begin to realise that everything is OK with you. You are able to look back on your life story with a deep respect and Fierce Love. You are able to see yourself for who you really are and

Fiercely Love what you see. You are able to see that your life is unfolding as it should. You are perfectly poised in life. You are ready to take the next step. You can take it with Fierce Love. You can and do make a difference in the world.

When you unleash your true potential in this way, the power of your resonance in the zero point field means that your words carry significant weight and gravitas. Your behaviour is completely in tune with your words and your sense of being. Everything adds up. You are highly convincing and influential. You are authentic. You are powerful. You are in it for yourself, the other party and the greater good of humanity and nature. You operate from the ultimate perspective so you know what is really important minus the egos. Not many people operate from this place. There is immense reward for you here.

There is nothing you need to resist. There is nothing you need to be for anyone else. There is nothing you need to push onto other people. The Fierce Love you hold for yourself and others is the only Love you will ever need.

You are perfectly poised. Everything that has been in your life is just perfect. You take the next perfect step in perfect harmony with the zero point field. You give and receive Fierce Love. You feel powerful as you act in harmony with the Oneness of the world and the ultimate future that is seeking to emerge.

- *What is holding you back from doing this in your life (a place, job, person, relationship or behaviour)?*
- *What will you do about that from a Fiercely Loving perspective?*
- *How will you use Fierce Love to transform that and move you past the blockage?*
- *What are you pretending not to know about?*
- *What does your soul yearn for?*
- *If there was no one to judge you, including yourself, what would you do differently in your life to unleash the power of your true potential?*

I believe that the time has come for you to unleash the power of that potential. It must remain latent in you no more.

Step forth.

Oneness

Once you take the One perspective and live your life by it, you see evidence of it all around you. Just like the paradigm shift that we talked about at the beginning of the book, once you adopt a new way of thinking, just as much evidence appears to back it up as did to back up the old way.

At the time of writing, it is two hundred years since Darwin's birth and one hundred and fifty years since he published his *Origin of Species* book. This was the birth of the theory of evolution. In a recent programme to celebrate these milestones, I saw Sir David Attenborough say to the camera the exact words, 'Everything is related'.[18]

If we look back in history to the very origin of our species, we see ancient shamans with inexplicable powers. Shamans studied nature closely and learned from it. They accessed different states of consciousness to gain guidance from animal spirit guides. Back then as a species we were inextricably linked to nature. We lived within it, day in, day out. We lived by its natural cycles. We were at One with our environment. We had to be. A lack of respect for the food or water sources often meant illness, hardship or death. Back then we knew the inescapable truth that nature was the greatest power.

The ego seeks separateness and definition; it wants to be separated from 'cavemen'. We like to be seen as superior to them. In many ways we are, but someone operating at the self-actualisation level is also able to see the wisdom in their ancient ways. They are able to take a more holistic view like the One perspective.

Shamans were aware of a power around them in the world that was difficult to define. Some felt as if they could communicate with it. Some could sense that it was conscious. Many claimed it was the ultimate power. The shamans saw spirits; other religions have called it god. God is a contentious issue right now. Richard Dawkins' *The God Delusion* was a best seller in 2007 and set about fundamentally dismantling any concept of a 'separate' god.[19]

In fact the concept of god is entirely dependent on your definition of it. I have heard many religious people define it as everything. God is in everything, between everything, in the spaces, in quiet moments, in joyous singing and somehow mysteriously in suffering and death too. God is a power. This power is omnipotent. It links all things. Could it be that thousands of years before the recent discoveries of quantum physics, people instinctively knew that everything was connected by some kind of inherent, omnipotent and loving energy?

If you define god as nothing more and nothing less than the spirit or energy in absolutely everything, then has science finally proved that definition of god? Would a definition of god that had to have something else, something separate, something different, something 'supernatural' be the ego talking? Have the countless quiet prayers and meditations over the years been a way of listening to the natural power of the zero point field? Have people with unwavering faith and Fierce Love been able to access the soul and its two-million-bit processor, thus enabling them to make a profound impact on the world?

The answers will depend on your beliefs. The One perspective gives religious believers, atheists, agnostics, scientists, people from all faiths and cultures a perspective that could unite them. With the One perspective everyone can be right, rather than us making others wrong. It's just a slightly different translation of the same thing. The One perspective can be a common platform upon which people can stand together to assess the situation. It is a platform that can enable people to make the kind of behavioural break-throughs that will bring about that utopian world described at the start.

Do you believe that is unrealistic or do you believe it is inevitable? Either way of course, you will be proved right. As always you have a choice. Today's paper reports that the Vatican has decided that Charles Darwin was on the right track when he claimed that man descended from the apes. On the 'other side', depending on your definition of god, science may have just proved that there is something out there after all. Science and religion are meeting. The spread of the One paradigm seems inevitable to me – it is already occurring.

With the One perspective, our ancient ancestors have profound lessons to teach us about the balance we strike in the natural world, both in our own lives and as a species as a whole. As we learn from the past and give it a useful relevance to our current world, ancient meets modern. The challenge is to evolve behaviourally to take into account what is natural for us individually and for our species as a whole, as well as living successfully in this day and age. If we can do that, then we stand a chance of preventing that dire WHO prediction coming true over the next few years. This is about change. It is about evolution. It is about progression. It is not about 'going back'.

A new paradigm is gradually emerging. It's coming. What is your role in all of this?

Self-actualisation

As you bring the One perspective down to a personal level, you are able to see that you are indeed a transmitter. Awareness of your iceberg and what that is bringing into your life can be incredibly refreshing. With awareness comes 90% of the solution and as you retune your frequency you are able to bring more of what your soul wants into your life.

You become less dependent on the things that drive the ego, like money, status, keeping up with the Joneses, competition, separation, definition, righteousness and judgement.

Life becomes a lot easier when you let go of all that. Things become more natural. You work with the natural grain of your wood. You spend more time collaborating with other people, races, species and your soul. The result is an approach of Fierce Love that as a way of life naturally grants people access to deep fulfilment, happiness and purpose every minute of every day.

You have to be ready for that behavioural evolution. You have to be ready to take on the ultimate adventure of mankind; finding and living your purpose. If you have not done the personal work, it lacks authenticity and power. It's not real. It's just another role for the ego to play. It requires some reflection in today's modern world and you will have to consciously choose to carve out that time. If you don't there is a danger that the WHO prediction will become personal (as it did with me) and you will be forced to. I was weak – I was pushed into it. You can be strong. You can read the signs and make a proactive choice to save you from that.

Clear the constant chattering of your ego and you are also able to be a receiver, receiving messages and information from the zero point field and your soul. You receive guidance and intuition that helps you to understand the journey that your soul wants to take. The journey is the point. It is not to 'arrive' anywhere, as a deep sense of purpose is likely to be bigger than your life, but you do celebrate passing through the stations along the way. You enjoy the journey with all its twists and turns. That's the point.

You owe it to yourself to live in the Real world and to live the life your soul wants to lead. You only have one crack at this thing called life; don't act out a play that someone else wants you to live. Live yours. If you listen carefully, receiving and transmitting in harmony, then you will bring your Real life to bear. It may not sit well with other people's egos or even yours. Remember that living a fulfilling life these days is a radical decision.

The reward is a life filled with Fierce Love, understanding and wisdom. The deep fulfilment, Fierce Love and soul-level happiness that results cannot be knocked by the ego. You develop tremendous self-confidence, power and influence balanced with curiosity, humility and Love.

I wish you this life.

My Part

One of the down sides of writing about something profound and universal is that if you know where to look, you can find that most of these ideas have been written about in some kind of format, but in different ways, for thousands of years. You could even say that there is actually only one story worth reading and it is this, it just appears in different guises whether in fact or fiction. I hope I have packaged it up in a simple way with some of my unique experiences to bring it to life in a practical and useful way for you.

I hope it brings some cutting-edge theories within easy reach of people who were unaware of them. I hope it will go some way to freeing people from the ego trap. I hope some people will use it to unleash the power of their true potential. I hope as a result that more people begin to feel as if they are on the 'right road'. I hope they will find that journey a more fulfilling, happier and more powerful place to be.

If this has been a 'pleasant read' for you, then of course I am happy about that; I hope that what you got from it was worth the time you invested reading it. Actually this book is not really very important in the big scheme of things. What really matters is what *you* do next. Often when I run leadership programmes I say, 'We can all have a lovely time over the next couple of days and learn lots of interesting things, but if you go away and do nothing different, it will have been a waste of everyone's time and money.'

So it is true of this book.

We both have a part to play in what happens next.

For my part, I travelled the world and have been lucky

enough to visit some places that many people only dream of going to. I have faced the nemesis of depression and come out of the other side. I have been trying to write this book in some kind of format for a decade now. I needed to find a different way of working to allow me the time to write this book and so I took a fundamental decision to set up my own business and not work full time. Over the last year since the 'knocking window' I have devoted hundreds of hours to writing it.

I have put a lot into this, but it has been hugely rewarding as it is part of the journey of what it seems I am here to do. This book represents part of my life purpose. It is a station along the way. I have written things in here that it is hard for me to say. My heart is in this book. I feel very vulnerable releasing it to people I do and don't know; people who could choose to ridicule it.

I also feel amazed that I have written this book. Most of the time it has actually felt as if something else has been writing it and that I have merely been a channel – tapping the keys obediently. I try to live the One perspective as much as possible. I have been listening to the zero point field. Your thoughts are in the zero point field. The common consciousness of mankind is in there. I have been listening to my intuition as a vehicle for accessing the thoughts, hopes and fears that we all release into the ether. If there is anything I have misinterpreted then it is entirely my fault, not the zero point field's. If I have translated anything incorrectly then it is my listening that needs to improve and I apologise.

This book is therefore made up of everything; including your thoughts. In a strange way, it feels to me as if the place that you are at in life has informed the book. If you have thought, 'That makes sense to me' at points in this book, it is because on one level I believe that you and others like you were helping to write what needed to be said. Your soul wanted this. But of course the zero point field is not limited only to our species. The broader world of all life including

202 • One: Changing the World from the Inside Out

animals and plants is in here too, all vibrating in the
moment; all asking that this be written.

The Oneness of the world helped me to write this book. It
therefore feels appropriate to honour that help and assistance. I therefore plan to set up a One Foundation and
through it donate a portion of the profits of this book to
'Oneful' projects. That just seems to be the natural thing to
do and of course nature is the greatest power.

I have attempted to write this book from a place of Fierce
Love. The main purpose is to spread awareness which leads
us to the final challenge. One night I was lying in bed considering what would be the ultimate Fiercely Loving thing to do
regarding the book and it hit me in a two-million-bit way.

I think there are plenty of people out there who talk a good
game, but don't live it – that fundamental difference between
level 2 and level 3 awareness. If I truly believe in what is written
in this book, the next step can not be driven purely by material
gain, it must be driven by my life purpose. As you know that is
to enable people to be the best they can be.

That led me to the final challenge that I put to you.

The Final Challenge

As I lay in bed that night, my soul told me that the ultimate
demonstration of Fierce Love concerning this book is for me
to challenge you to give it away to a complete stranger. Not
only is this the perfect thing to do from a Oneful, Fiercely
Loving perspective, but it could also help you to unleash
some of the power of your true potential.

You may feel that the book was OK, but you don't buy into
all of it. In this case there is nothing to lose by giving it away.
In fact the only reason not to pass it on would be if you felt
extremely negatively about the views expressed in this book
and wanted to suppress what it had to offer. If that is the case
then you would be right to burn it or stick it on a shelf to
gather dust.

On the other hand, if you have enjoyed the book, if it resonated with you, then there is a chance that you may have put some of the ideas into practice and seen some real, tangible results. Your ego may not want to part with it. But if you got something from it and you want to live in a more Oneful world, then the best way to help others join you there and contribute to your life in a Oneful way would be to grant others the same awareness. Although you may love this book and not want to part with it on an ego level, taking the One perspective, what better thing to do then than give the book away and drive awareness?

If you hand this on, then others are likely to do the same. The physical book you are holding in your hands has the potential to set off on its own journey. It may pass through many people's hands thanks to your decision. Other people will read this book and think back to the moment a stranger gave it to them. They will thank you. They will be more likely to do the same.

Some of the world's resources have been used to create the physical book that you are holding. What better thing to do than to recycle them immediately, enabling someone else to make use of them by being able to read it without having to use up more by buying another book? As soon as you give it away it becomes 100% recycled. When the next person gives it away it becomes 200% recycled. What a great use of the world's resources.

If you give it to a stranger, you 'seed' a person who may not normally choose to read a book like this. You give someone a chance to gain awareness that they may not normally have gained. If the time is right for them, they will want to thank you in the future and you will feel that in the zero point field. They are likely to do the same, thus seeding other areas.

You have the chance to talk about this book with your friends and relatives. As a result of how you talk about the book and its ideas, they may choose to buy a copy. Of course it would be inappropriate to forcibly push the ideas in this book down other people's throats. Be aware that everyone has an iceberg

204 • *One: Changing the World from the Inside Out*

and some people are not ready for life's ultimate journey.

The most influential thing you can do is to develop level 3 awareness of your life purpose. Live, breathe and resonate in that space of self-actualisation. Let your soul sparkle. That is catching. It may be that this book could become a talking point between you and friends. It could become an easy reference point that enables you to discuss some of the more important things in life.

Do you ever get fed up with the same old shallow conversations? Do you ever wish you could have a deeper discussion about some of the questions posed in this book, but not know how to bring them up? In my experience when I talk about the book most people are fascinated and we have a fantastic discussion. If you take the first step, you have the potential to have some amazing conversations.

You may think, 'I want to re-read this book! I haven't completed all the exercises.' I often feel like this when I finish a book. I can honestly say that to date I have not got round to doing it yet with any book. The time has passed. Trust that you got what you needed from the book this time round and if there is more for you, then at a later date the zero point field will generate that opportunity. Maybe you will be given a copy for your birthday. Maybe a stranger will hand it to you. Maybe you will chose to buy another copy when you feel you need it.

You may have parted with money to buy this book and think, 'Why should I give it away to a stranger?' If that is the case, then you have not grasped some of the key learnings of this book. You are likely to find it difficult to unleash the power of your true potential from here. Try it. See what happens. I think you will be pleasantly surprised by how it makes you feel and the lessons you could learn from it.

It is a great way for you to demonstrate a real tangible step on the road to unleashing the power of your true potential. No matter what you decide to do differently or otherwise in your life personally, by setting this book off on its own journey of purpose you will play an integral part in spreading awareness of the One paradigm.

It's Not Goodbye

This book was written from the perspective of a free spirit. It was highly intuitive. It feels to me as if it has wings and wants to fly. Its future will be determined by the natural systems of human interaction. You and the zero point field will take care of what happens next. Of course you will decide whether you set it off on its way to achieve its true potential or whether you hold it back. Of course whatever you do will be just perfect for the place you are at on your journey and that is truly fine at a deep level.

Although this is the end of this book, of course it is not the end of the journey. It could be just the beginning for you. People have been predicting a landslide of human consciousness for a while now. What you do with this book has the potential to stop this being a prediction and instead to deliver it in a real, tangible way. It would be great to be a part of that change in history wouldn't it? It could be an important step in saving us from ourselves.

There is a log in the back of this book. If you like you could write your name in it. If you bought this book, then yours will be the first name. You will be the one who can set it off on its journey through the hands of a string of readers. If you are further down the list you will be able to see the tangible proliferation of a Oneful approach as people show that they are ready to do something that flies in the face of the modern world way. You will have been handed the book by a long-lost relative. The more people you see on the list, the more tangible the fact that people are looking for an alternative way. The more you can see that people just like you and me are ready to try something different.

If you are interested in the themes in this book and want to stay in touch, go to: www.theoneperspective.com. This will also be a place to keep up to date with Oneful news. I will post details about the activities the One Foundation has helped to fund (we are able to put twice as much into the foundation for any book purchased from this website). You can look at that and be proud that you are an integral part of it all. I would also love to hear from you if this book has helped you in any way. You already know that enabling you to fulfil your true potential is my life purpose and hearing about real tangible examples is therefore hugely rewarding for me.

So take a look around you. Who does your intuition say wants to read this book right now? Trust your two-million-bit processor. Consider what you are going to say to them, because it is not normal in the modern world paradigm of scarcity to give things away to strangers. From the One perspective however it is a normal and healthy way of re-uniting with a long-lost relative of yours. Of course they may not be aware of that yet.

Thank you for reading the book.

I wish you all the best on the rest of your journey.

Now I challenge you to adopt a perspective of Fierce Love and give it away to one of your distant relatives.

Acknowledgements

Acebird: co-creator and editor of this book. World-class coach and crucible, most incisive critic, greatest supporter, unwavering believer and soul mate. It really would not have come to pass without you on so many levels. Thanks for providing the time, support, input and challenge that has made this what it is and for championing me throughout the highs and the lows.

Bev Knox MCC for getting me really excited about my life purpose.

Clients for sharing with me what was beneath the surface of your icebergs and for the courage you showed when making deep transformational change. Living a fulfilling life is a radical decision. You make my job a privilege.

CTI classmates (Alun, Ann, Anna, Caroline, Deby, Elaine, Helen, Jenny, Jo, Judy, Lee-Anne, Leo, Mark, Mary, Muna, Natasha, Rosie, Ruth, Sarah, Steve, Sue, Tiffany and Virginia) for practising on me and allowing me to practise on you. You are a special group of people and helped to give birth to this.

Eagle for the transformational energy of 2009.

Ellen Fredericks MCC for your support, championing and coaching throughout this project; you are a very dear friend.

Ellie for being the tiger cub that fills my spaces and for your wonderful teachings.

Gwen and Derek Thurley for their open-mindedness, curiosity and support.

Kate Burton for coaching me during in the early stages of this book and asking me the awkward questions that I didn't want to answer.

Iceberg Coaching for a deep appreciation of the inherent power that is beneath the surface for everyone and for enabling people to unleash it daily.

Lynne Sibley (Jana) for a magnificent introduction to shamanism and the ancient wisdom of our ancestors.

Leading Initiatives Worldwide (especially Simon, Jane, Farren and the Marks) for a fantastic relationship and for the many assignments that have helped me to evolve.

Matt H (The Gaffer) for your wonderful brotherhood and for bringing some cutting edge scientific theories within my reach.

Matt Round for his patience and understanding in designing the cover and website.

Miles Bailey for sharing his experience and insight from the publishing world with honesty and integrity.

Mouse (6 in 6 days) for showing me what was under my nose.

Moose for being my power animal and for providing so many useful teachings in the space between consciousness and unconsciousness.

Mum and Dad for my safe and nurturing upbringing. You gave me the foundation upon which to build a life that enabled this.

Milne Kiltner MCC for nailing me (I have been 'Milned').

Potential Squared (especially Colin, Paul, Mike, Adie and Synchronous Milda) for a fantastic relationship that has enabled me to develop and for the clients that have provided so much experience of icebergs.

Raven for the snow and company when alone in the mountains.

Rob for being down to earth, strong, loyal and honest at all times.

Sam for being the catalyst that enabled me to silence the gremlins and for all your wonderful teachings.

Spider for looking out for me.

Starbucks St Albans and its warm, smiley manager Sophie for a friendly 'third place' to write.

Susy Southgate for sending me on the Vision Quest that gave me direction when I was at a significant crossroads in my life.

Tony Barton PCC for the quote that touched me and set me up to do something different.

Tiger for his immense power and energy and for allowing me to take out an overdraft when I needed to.

Tobes for the long discussions about Love over a beer.

Vivster for being a vivacious innovator and for applying such energy when bringing One to life. Thank you for your mindful project management and speed to action.

You (the reader) for contributing to the future that was seeking to emerge (I hope I listened properly to what you wanted) and for investing your precious time in reading this book. I also thank you for what you are about to do.

Zero Point Field for everything.

Notes

1. See www.who.int/mental_health/management/depression/ definition/en/.
2. Laura Clark and Andy Dolan, the *Daily Mail*, 20 June 2007, quoting a report from the Office of National Statistics.
3. Abraham Maslow in Laurie J. Mullins, *Management and Organisational Behaviour* (Pitman Publishing 1996).
4. See http://en.wikipedia.org/wiki/Alain_Aspect.
5. Lynne McTaggart, *The Field*, Element, 2003.
6. United Nations report, 24 May 2005. See www.cnn.com/2005/US /02/24/un.population/index.html.
7. Ahmed Djoghlaf in Fergus Beely and Rosamund Kidman Cox (eds), *Planet Earth: The Future*, BBC Books, 2006.
8. National Institute of Mental Health. See www.nimh.nih.gov.
9. E.O. Wilson in *Planet Earth: The Future.*
10. Richard Mabey in *Planet Earth: The Future.*
11. *The Scientist*, vol. 18, issue 13.
12. Robert May in *Planet Earth: The Future.*
13. Susan Scott, *Fierce Conversations*, Berkley Books, 2004.
14. Lynne McTaggart, *The Field*, pp. 138-41.
15. Susan Scott, *Fierce Conversations*, Berkley Books, 2004.
16. Gill Edwards, *Wild Love*, Piatkus Books Ltd, 2006.
17. Diagram from Peter Senge, C. Otto Scharmer, Joseph Jaworski and Betty Sue Flowers, *Presence: Human Purpose and the Field of the Future*, Nicholas Brealey Publishing, 2005.
18. *Charles Darwin and the Tree of Life*. See www.bbc.co.uk /programmes/b00hd5mf.
19. Richard Dawkins, *The God Delusion*, Black Swan, 2007.

Bibliography

Beely, Fergus and Rosamund Kidman Cox (eds), *Planet Earth: The Future*, BBC Books, 2006

Brehony, Kathleen A., *Awakening at Midlife*, Riverhead Books, 1996

Dawkins, Richard, *The God Delusion*, Black Swan, 2007

Dyer, Dr Wayne W., *Inspiration: Your Ultimate Calling*, Hay House, 2006

Edwards, Gill, *Wild Love: Discover the Magical Secrets of Freedom, Joy and Unconditional Love*, Piatkus, 2006

Farmer, Steven D., *Animal Spirit Guides*, Hay House, 2006

Goffee, Rob and Jones, Gareth, *Why Should Anyone Be Led by You?*, Harvard Business School Press, 2006

Jaworski, Joseph, *Synchronicity: The Inner Path of Leadership*, Berrett-Koehler Publishers 1998

McTaggart, Lynne, *The Field*, Element, 2003

Mullins, Laurie J., *Management and Organisational Behaviour*, Pitman Publishing, 1996

Pink, Dan H., *A Whole New Mind: Why Right-Brainers Will Rule the Future*, Penguin, 2006

Scott, Susan, *Fierce Conversations*, Berkley Books, 2004

Senge, Peter, Scharmer, C. Otto, Jaworski, Joseph and Flowers, Betty Sue, *Presence: Human Purpose and the Field of the Future*, Nicholas Brealey Publishing, 2005

Tolle, Eckhart, *The Power of Now*, Hodder and Stoughton, 2005

Tolle, Eckhart, *A New Earth*, Penguin Books, 2005

Whitworth, Laura, Kimsey-House, Henry and Sandahl, Phil, *Co-Active Coaching: New Skills for Coaching People Toward Success in Work and Life*, Davies-Black Publishing, 1998

Log

Name	Date	Comments

Name	Date	Comments

About the Author

Noj Hinkins (Author)

Noj's love of variety and adventure has taken him to the seven continents of the world. From trekking in the Himalayas and kayaking through the brash ice of Antarctica to studying active volcanoes and traversing the deserts of Australia, he has come face to face with the natural world and its indigenous people. The links and similarities between such a diverse range of habitats and people helped formulate the basic principles of the One perspective.

Noj is a consultant and coach, facilitating leadership programmes and team-building sessions for a diverse range of organisations including governments, schools, charities and corporations across Europe, the USA and Africa.

Noj is married with two children. In his spare time he enjoys being a dad, writing, trekking and ornithology.

Liz Blossom (Co-Creator and Editor)

Liz is passionate about people. From an early age she was fascinated by human behaviour and her degree in pyschology developed this initial spark into a desire to understand what makes human beings successful in life. Liz has gone on to make a career as a coach and her purpose on a professional level is to enable people to fulfil their true potential. Doing this with capble, courageous individuals and witnessing their exceptional results gives her real happiness and fulfilment.

On a personal level, Liz loves singing, travel and the 'great outdoors' and gets much of her energy from having adventures and new experiences. Her latest expedition was a husky sledding safari in the Arctic Circle. Liz has a husband and two young children with whom she loves to spend time, so creating a healthy work/life balance is very important to her.

Liz and Noj are partners of Iceberg Coaching, a business that delivers transformational 'beneath the surface' change to enable people and organisations to unleash the power of their true potential.

Lightning Source UK Ltd.
Milton Keynes UK
22 September 2010
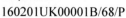
160201UK00001B/68/P